THE
MAYOR AND THE JUDGE

THE INSIDE STORY OF
THE WAR AGAINST COVID

JUDGE NELSON W. WOLFF
FOREWORD BY MAYOR RON NIRENBERG

Special notice: Under the contract with Elm Grove Publishing all royalties that would normally go to the author will instead be paid directly to the Hidalgo Foundation that provides grants to Bexar County for our Bibilotech, historic restoration and childrens' programs.

Cover painting "Masked Defenders of the Alamo City" ©2020 Sara Barcus used with kind permission of the artist. *www.sarabarcus.com*

ISBN: 978-1-943492-93-0 (Hardback)
ISBN: 978-1-943492-92-3 (Soft Cover)
ISBN: 978-1-943492-94-7 (eBook)

Publisher's Cataloging-in-Publication Data
provided by Five Rainbows Cataloging Services

Names: Wolff, Nelson W., 1940- author. | Nirenberg, Ron, writer of foreword.
Title: The mayor and the judge : the inside story of the war against COVID / Judge Nelson W. Wolff ; foreword by Mayor Ron Nirenberg.
Description: San Antonio, TX : Elm Grove Publishing, 2022. | Includes index.
Identifiers: ISBN 978-1-943492-93-0 (hardcover) | ISBN 978-1-943492-92-3 (paperback) | ISBN 978-1-943492-94-7 (ebook)
Subjects: LCSH: Mayors--Texas--San Antonio--Biography. | COVID-19 Pandemic, 2020---United States. | COVID-19 Pandemic, 2020---Political aspects--United States. | COVID-19 (Disease)-- Political aspects--United States. | San Antonio (Tex.)--Politics and government. | United States-- Politics and government--21st century. | BISAC: POLITICAL SCIENCE / American Government / Local. | POLITICAL SCIENCE / Public Policy / Health Care. | SOCIAL SCIENCE / Disease & Health Issues. | BIOGRAPHY & AUTOBIOGRAPHY / Political.
Classification: LCC RA644.C67 W65 2022 (print) | LCC RA644.C67 (ebook) | DDC 362.1962414--dc23.

Book design by designpanache

ELM GROVE PUBLISHING
San Antonio, Texas, USA
www.elmgrovepublishing.com

Elm Grove Publishing is a legally registered trade name of Panache Communication Arts, Inc.

CONTENTS

Foreword by Mayor Ron Nirenberg........................9

1. Coronavirus Arms Up........................15

2. Blunting The First Attack........................29

3. Unilateral Disarmament........................62

4. Summertime Tsunami........................76

5. Fall-Time Complacency........................103

6. Wintertime Eruption of 2020–2021........................119

7. Springtime Renewal........................147

8. Surprise Attack of The Delta Force........................162

9. Out of Africa—Omicron........................192

10. The Coming of the Unborn Virus........................207

History of COVID-19 Patients in San Antonio
Area Hospitals 3/12/2020–2/10/2022........................224

Acknowledgments........................226

References and Sources........................228

Index........................232

To my loving wife, Tracy,
who supported our family throughout the pandemic.

Foreword
by Mayor Ron Nirenberg

"WE ARE ALL IN THIS TOGETHER."

What started as a catchphrase to remind everyone about their role in combating what would become a global pandemic, has emerged as an eternal truth about our human condition.

A person's choice to wear a mask or get vaccinated—or not—can break—or perpetuate—the chain of transmission of a deadly virus. What happens to any one of us—for good or ill—reverberates throughout the entire community.

This clarity, above all else, is what I hope we have regained from the pain of the globe's most terrible ongoing crisis in a generation.

When we look back, each of us will assess what we did during our prolonged collective battle against COVID-19. From the nurse in the Intensive Care Unit, to the grocery store clerk helping a panicked customer, to the teacher figuring out how to instruct six-year-olds through a computer screen, to the paramedic transporting a COVID-stricken patient to the hospital and hoping not to transport the virus back home to her family, we each have a

COVID-19 journey worthy of reflection.

Through the last 19 months, as mayor of the seventh largest city in the United States, it has been an honor to go on this journey with my counterpart, Nelson Wolff, and in the following pages, you will experience his detailed account of how the two of us fought the spread of COVID-19 through our community.

As mayor of the city of San Antonio, I had the privilege of working side-by-side with Judge Wolff—often seven days a week—through this traumatic episode in our civic and personal lives.

The time of COVID-19 was one filled with an abundance of emotion, confusion, and questions—many remaining unanswered. We each will leave this experience with our own points of view about not only what happened, but what we did, what we learned, and who we became as a result.

In this book, Judge Wolff takes the reader through his journey and his view of what, as Bexar County's top administrative executive, he could control, what he could defy, and what he could ultimately leave behind.

This book will inspire you to reflect on your own story just as I am thinking about my own.

I remember in April 2020, as the magnitude of the pandemic just became clear, being asked by *San Antonio Express-News* Editorial Page Editor Josh Brodesky, "What keeps you up at night?"

My mind went to the photo taken a few weeks earlier by veteran *Express-News* photographer William Luther of the staggering lines of cars filled with residents seeking food at a San Antonio Food Bank mass distribution site on the south side of San Antonio. That image, an aerial shot of the sea of cars which got reprinted and reproduced in *The New York Times* and publications and TV shows across the nation, was transcendent.

Some 120,000 families in a week's time—twice as many as in the days prior to COVID-19—needed food donations to feed their families. That meant that in my community, where we had 3 percent unemployment, where major employers were relocating their headquarters, where the economy had some of the best momentum in a generation, 60,000 families each week still would be unable to put food on the table if not for the charity of the San Antonio Food Bank.

But that is not just San Antonio's story. That picture was America. In our new gilded age of economic disparity and segregation, millions of American families were one event—a health event, a lost job, an accident, a pandemic—away from economic devastation, and many others were already there. COVID-19 became that event for those millions.

My answer to Brodesky's question of what keeps me up at night is the same today as it was in April 2020. I hope we are not content to go back to the way things were: that same "normal" that had so many millions of Americans so close to the brink.

In San Antonio, we have dedicated ourselves to coming back better, stronger, more resilient, and more equitable. Voters saw the need and approved SA Ready to Work, a four-year $154 million workforce development program, with the goal of lifting tens of thousands of San Antonio residents to more stable, prosperous careers. We are making strategic investments across sectors, geographies, and policy areas to break cycles of generational poverty that have gripped our community for far too long.

Ultimately, what COVID-19 has taught us all is that we have an individual responsibility to contribute to the common good. And during a time when our behavior as individual citizens, neighbors, and family members would affect other people's lives, it is my greatest hope as mayor during this time that we will walk away from this not only feeling responsibility, courage, and sadness, but that we can share those stories with each other like Nelson has done in the following pages.

And as I reflect on my own journey throughout COVID-19, I know that this time has been challenging, especially the tightrope act of balancing not only what we can do as individuals but also what we should do as a community.

I will also look back at this era as a time in which I got to know and understand what was in Judge Wolff's heart, the discerning leadership, and what was driving him as he began to wrap up 50 years of public service during a time of such instability.

I enjoyed the quiet moments that we had together as well as the larger bombastic ones, defending our community against the recklessness of state and federal officials. We grew in mutual admiration for each other while we toiled to lead the county and city, respectively, and made some of the most difficult and important decisions of our lives.

As Judge Wolff takes you down the journey of his experiences, observations, and decisions during this time, you will no doubt reflect on your own journey as well.

Judge Wolff's insights and recollections of the pandemic from the center of the struggle to contain the deadly virus that wracked our community offers his inside view of our community's path forward through the most difficult crisis of our lives.

Ron Nirenberg

"Masked Defenders of the Alamo City" by Sara Barcus.

1. Coronavirus Arms Up

I DID NOT PAY TOO MUCH ATTENTION when on December 16, 2019, a doctor at Hubei Provincial Hospital in Wuhan, China, a city of 12 million people, reported a patient that had flu-like symptoms and a follow-up scan showed that it was a new form of pneumonia. Instead, I was caught up with the debacle in Washington, watching the House of Representatives impeach President Donald Trump.

A few days later, on December 27, a finding at a Chinese lab showed that the virus was not the flu, but instead said it was a virus similar to the SARS-CoV 2002-03, which stands for severe acute respiratory syndrome coronavirus.

While Chinese officials remained quiet about the finding, doctors began to secretly warn people over social media about what they were seeing in their patients.

Before SARS-CoV 2002-03 no one had ever heard of a coronavirus virus causing severe illness in people. However, those infected by SARS-CoV 2002-03 had various symptoms including high fever, headache, body aches, diarrhea, and mild respiratory symptoms. It was spread by people who had symptoms in close person-to-person contact through droplets, such as a cough or sneeze, or airborne through fine particles of aerosol. It spread slowly because people who are sick usually stay home, acting as a break on transmission. Generally, a person with SARS infected a few other people with SARS. Consequently, it spread to only 29 countries and was contained within nine months, ending in July 2003.

SARS-CoV 2002-03 was also more severe, progressing to pneumonia and having a higher fatality rate. Because the virus' spread was slow and contained, it only resulted in 8,000 becoming infected and 777 confirmed deaths, but likely many more died that were not reported.

Twelve years later another outbreak of respiratory syndrome coronavirus occurred in South Korea: Middle East Respiratory Syndrome (MERS). This virus was first identified in 2012 in Saudi Arabia and was also spread by symptomatic people. There were even fewer cases this time: 2,000 cases worldwide resulting in 600 deaths.

I was less concerned when the virus was identified as a coronavirus family member rather than a new strain of flu. History had shown coronaviruses to be less threating than any strain of flu we had seen.

The question of where the virus originated came under intense debate. Chinese officials believed it originated from the Wuhan wet market where live animals are slaughtered and sold. But early on suspicion arose about a possible leak from the Wuhan Institute of Virology, China's foremost coronavirus research facility.

The research lab is located about seven miles away from the Wuhan wet market. It has one of the world's largest repositories of bat samples and a data base of 22,000 viral samples. The SARS-CoV 2002-03 outbreak was linked to bats.

Bats, which make up one-fifth of all mammals, are a large

and mobile group of potential disease spreaders. Bats are also popular as food and medicine in China. Dr. Shi Zhenbgli, a scientist at the Wuhan lab known as the "bat woman," had experience in searching bat caves to find the source of SARS-CoV 2002-03.

The Wuhan lab has biosafety labs classified as biosafety level two (BSL-2) and biosafety level three (BLS-3). Research on coronaviruses is done in BSL-3 labs where agents are studied that may cause serious or potentially lethal disease through inhalation. All laboratory personnel are provided medical surveillance and offered relevant immunizations. Researchers must cover their front with protective clothing and then discard and decontaminate after each use. They have a restricted entrance with a separate door from other areas of building. They must also have two sets of self-closing doors.

United States experts had visited the lab in 2017 and 2018 and warned about sub-par safety standards. Viruses had escaped from Chinese labs four times previously, including SARS from the National Institute of Virology in Beijing.

The experts also noticed that gain of function research was being conducted in the Wuhan lab. In gain of function research, the scientists manipulate the virus to see if they can increase transmission to humans. The purpose of the theory is to then develop a vaccine for the new mutation. Many in the scientific community called it "looking for a gas leak with a lighted match."

In the United States, scientists have debated the gain of function since at least 2011 when virologists genetically modified H5NI avian-flu virus so it could spread among ferrets contained in the lab. In 2014 the federal government imposed a pause on such research with certain dangerous viruses, developed a set of rules, and allowed some research to continue.

Over the next two years the source of the virus would continue to be a mystery as China put obstacles in the way of international inspection. But most scientists believe the virus jumped from an animal at the wet market because most who were sick had visited a section where live raccoon dogs, which carry coronaviruses, were sold. No one has ever been able to pinpoint the source of the SARS-CoV 2002-03, and we probably will never know for sure where COVID-19 originated.

As January 2020 rolled around, the World Health Organization (WHO) did not seem too concerned about the event in China even though the virus began to spread to other parts of the country. More people were getting sick, including doctors and nurses, but Chinese officials continued to say there was no evidence of human-to-human transmission. WHO accepted the official Chinese version. However, concern started to grow around the world as an outbreak was feared.

***

Once you identify the virus then hopefully a vaccine can be developed. To understand a virus, the first step is to obtain a genomic sequence of it, a sort of DNA blueprint of what makes the virus unique. On January 5, 2020, Chinese labs had established a sequence, and five days later, on January 10, they released the information.

By January 20 the virus had spread to Japan, South Korea, and Thailand. On the same day a Chinese medical expert stated on television that the virus was transmissible between humans. The next day the first case in the United States was reported in Washington State. This person had recently returned from China.

On January 23, the world took notice when we woke up

to the news that China had begun a lockdown on the city of Wuhan, affecting 56 million people. WHO called the virus spread a public health emergency of international concern (PHEIC) which is essentially a way of saying that this is something that could become a pandemic. A potential international spread of the disease could happen and would require a coordinated international response. WHO later named the disease COVID-19 after the virus that caused it and the year it was discovered.

Five days later after WHO announced the PHEIC, Centers for Disease Control and Prevention (CDC) Director Nancy Meissonier stated that they thought COVID-19 was a low risk in the United States because only people with symptoms spread SARS-CoV and MERS and neither of these coronaviruses posed a major threat.

Presidential Medical Advisor Dr. Anthony Fauci, the United States' leading epidemiologist, said it would be unusual for asymptomatic persons to drive an epidemic. Fauci was the director of the National Institute of Allergy and Infectious Diseases and had been the medical advisor to every president since Ronald Reagan. He would have many challenges ahead as advisor to President Trump.

While COVID-19 was picking up steam, we listened to the impeachment trial of President Trump that was happening in the United States Senate. On February 5 the Senate voted 52–48 along party lines to find Trump not guilty of abuse of power.

The impeachment was a waste of time without any bipartisan support. The impeachment would eventually prove to be advantageous to Trump.

***

During my tenure as County Judge, I had developed a good working relationship with five different mayors of San Antonio. We would meet either weekly or biweekly to discuss the issues we were facing. Together we have created numerous partnerships on various capital projects. We have also avoided duplication of services by contracting with each other. If we cannot come to an agreement on issues, then we go separate ways without criticizing each other. Well, most of the time.

I was now working with San Antonio Mayor Ron Nirenberg who had just won his re-election to his second two-year term in May of 2019. During his first term we had difficulties getting along, but after his re-election he became more consistent and assertive in his leadership and our relationship become much better. It would prove to be critical as we approached what would become a pandemic. We would have to be a strong team willing to make controversial decisions and stick to them, no matter the political consequences.

Without any notice to Nirenberg or myself, on February 5, 2020, the CDC announced that a plane carrying 91 Americans from Wuhan, China, was headed to Joint Base San Antonio-Lackland. Two days later 91 American citizens who had been in Wuhan, China, landed at Lackland Air Force Base located on the southwest side of San Antonio. On the same day that evacuees landed, Li Wenliang, the Chinese doctor who was reprimanded for leaking a lab report, died of COVID-19.

The evacuees included American citizens, residents, and their family members who had been in China. They would be quarantined for 14 days, enough time for COVID-19 symptoms, such as coughing, fever, and fatigue, to emerge. Six days later one evacuee tested positive.

Ten days later, on February 17, 144 passengers from the

Diamond Princess cruise ship were flown into San Antonio and quarantined on the base as well. The *Diamond Princess* had a COVID-19 outbreak among its 3,700 passengers and crew after it had departed from the Port of Yokohama on January 20 for a tour through southeast Asia.

While the *Diamond Princess* was quarantined for 14 days off the coast of Yokohama, 454 people were infected by the time the evacuees arrived in San Antonio. The virus spread quickly on board the ship because so many people were confined in close quarters. It was the first example of how mass gatherings could become super-spreader events. The most alarming aspect of this was that none of the people on board had been in Wuhan.

Three days after the arrival of the *Diamond Princess*, the original group of evacuees, save for one COVID-19-positive evacuee, was released to go home.

On February 17, I participated in a conference call with Harris County Judge Lina Hidalgo, Travis County Judge Sara Eckhardt, Dallas County Judge Clay Jenkins, Tarrant County Judge Glenn Whitley, and El Paso County Judge Ricardo Samaniego. Between Harris, Dallas, Tarrant, Travis, El Paso, and Bexar County, we represented 51 percent of the citizens of Texas.

I told them our concerns about the evacuees possibly spreading COVID-19 into our community. We discussed measures we would take if an outbreak did occur. Throughout the pandemic, we would continue to communicate and keep each other up to date on what was happening in our communities.

At the same time Nirenberg began conference calls with the mayors of the major cities located in the above five counties. Between the two of us we picked up valuable information from our peers around the state.

***

As we began to get organized for a possible pandemic, I thought back to the last time that our community had faced a deadly virus. In September 2014, a Liberian national had traveled to Dallas (300 miles from San Antonio) on September 20 and four days later succumbed to Ebola. Ebola is a deadly virus that was first discovered in 1976 in the Democratic Republic of the Congo.

We were fortunate to have officials from Texas Biomedical Research Institute (Texas Biomed) join our team that Bexar County Office of Emergency Management had assembled. Texas Biomed is the only independent non-profit infectious disease research institution in the United States with an 80-year history of dedication to eradicating infections around the world. They partner with more than 30 companies and academic partners.

They have the only privately owned biosafety level four lab (BSL-4) in the country, where they study agents at high risk of aerosol transmission that are frequently fatal, have no available vaccine or treatments, and have an unknown transmission risk.

Ebola was among the most dangerous viruses they had conducted research on. They had the credibility to assure our citizens that the only way they could contact Ebola was through direct contact with the blood or body fluids of an infected person or through needles and syringes.

Our team of health experts held a press conference on October 15, 2014, to explain the threat and our preparedness. I stated it was highly unlikely that we would have a case of Ebola, but we needed to be prepared to respond effectively. Health officials stated that people should avoid contact with patients exposed to Ebola, not handle items that have been in contact, and wear protective clothing if around an Ebola patient.

Dallas contained any spread, and we never had an Ebola case in San Antonio so the incident was quickly forgotten. But COVID-19 would not be so easy to contain because it would spread through the air from droplets or small particles of aerosol from the infected person.

As concern about the COVID-19 threat grew, Mayor Nirenberg and I assembled a team of experts much like we did during the Ebola threat. We met at the Southwest Texas Regional Advisory Council's (STRAC's) office on February 21. Led by Eric Epley, STRAC coordinates patient flow to over 70 hospitals in 27 Texas counties surrounding Bexar County. The first COVID meeting of health care officials at STRAC headquarters was on February 21, 2020.

The first COVID meeting of health care officials at STRAC headquarters on February 21, 2020.

As we gathered our health care leaders to prepare for a possible outbreak of COVID-19, we looked to three institutions as the major players: the Bexar County Hospital District doing business as University Health System (UHS), the University of Texas Health Science Center (UT Health), and San Antonio Metropolitan Health District (Metro Health). They would be the key institutions that Mayor Nirenberg and I would count on in preparing for the pandemic.

UHS is the teaching hospital for UT Health. The Commissioners Court appoints the seven-member board of managers, of which I appoint three. We also set their budget, tax rate, and debt issuance. George Hernandez, the president of UHS, presides over 9,000 employees and a sprawling network of clinics, research institutes, and outpatient surgery centers as well as our new hospital and clinical building that the Commissioners Court funded.

Dr. William Henrich is the president of UT Health and oversees the schools of medicine, dentistry, nursing, health professionals, and the graduate school of biomedical research. Over 6,000 people work for UT Health.

In 1966 the City of San Antonio and Bexar County entered into an agreement to create the San Antonio Metropolitan Health District, which was responsible for providing public health programs in the city and unincorporated areas of Bexar County. Most of the 26 suburban cities in Bexar County have since also joined the health district.

Metro Health is a department within the city with the director appointed by the City Manager. Their services include health code enforcement, food inspections, environmental monitoring, health education, emergency preparedness, and, most importantly, communicable disease control. In addition to UHS, UT Health, and Metro Health we had other major health care systems that would be critical in addressing the COVID-19 pandemic.

Brooke Army Medical Center, located on the Ft. Sam

Houston military base, is a teaching hospital for military medical residents. They sustain over 60 accredited education programs including 25 graduate medical education programs. They were a major player in virus research; vaccines can be developed in their state-of-the-art military hospital.

The Audie Murphy Memorial Veterans' Hospital is a comprehensive care facility for veterans, a Level 11 research center that includes aging, cancer, diabetes, and HIV research, and a teaching hospital for UT Health. We also have three major privately owned hospital systems. They include Baptist Health System led by CEO Matthew Stone, Christus Santa Rosa led by CEO Dean Alexander, and Methodist Healthcare led by CEO Allen Harrison.

Texas Biomedical Research Institute, overseen by President Larry Schlesinger, has 65 PhD scientists and 300 staff members working on hundreds of scientific projects each year. In addition to the BSL-4 lab where they did research on Ebola, they also have six BSL-3 labs where they research viruses such as coronaviruses.

Our health care institutions and biotechnology firms collaborate on various research projects including integrated biomedicine, cellular therapeutics, genetics, virology, and immunology. Together the research projects total $900 million annually.

As of 2020, San Antonio's health and bioscience industry had created over 200,000 jobs, employing nearly one in five workers locally, and generated $42.4 billion in revenue. In the past decade, the industry has increased its economic impact by 74 percent. We had a vibrant health care industry in San Antonio that was ready to meet any challenge that came our way.

At our first meeting of health care leaders, we all agreed that the exposed quarantined Americans should not leave the base. We went over safety measures to contain any spread of the virus if someone were to become infected in San Antonio. We began identifying hospital beds and looking for personal protective equipment (PPE) for medical personnel.

On the same day, Nirenberg and I met with Admiral Brett P. Giroir, the assistant secretary for at the U.S. Department of Health and Human Services (HHS). We expressed our concern about the evacuees being transported to off-site hospitals for testing and observation for mild systems. We followed up with a letter to Secretary of Defense Mark Esper demanding that they not send the quarantine citizens out into our community.

Following our meeting Nirenberg called our congressional delegation asking for help and telling them we needed personal protective equipment for health care workers. He also asked them to put pressure on federal agencies to adopt protocols that prevent the evacuees from transmitting COVID-19 into the general population.

I wrote a letter to Congressman Chip Roy asking for his help in requiring the CDC to collect samples for testing and monitor patients on base rather than sending them to hospitals and exposing our citizens to COVID-19. He followed up with a letter to HHS Director Alex Azar and U.S. Secretary of Defense Mark Esper asking several questions. Neither one of us got a satisfactory response.

I felt better when I received a call from the CDC saying they would use their Center for Domestic Preparedness in Anniston, Alabama, for any additional evacuees. On February 22, I received an e-mail from the HHS Director of Intergovernmental and External Affairs verifying that information.

It never happened. Alabama Senator Richard Shelby blocked the transfer. He stated that he did it to ensure the safety of Alabamians. Smart guy.

Four days later, on February 26, the CDC confirmed the

first community-spread COVID-19 case in United States. That meant that someone who had not been out of the country had caught COVID-19 from another citizen. On the same day CDC Director Dr. Nancy Meissonier stated that the agency is "preparing as if we are going to see community spread in the near term." This was an alarming statement considering a month earlier on January 28 she said COVID-19 was a low risk. I made a comment to the media that we had better expect that things are going to get worse.

At the same time, the first death outside of China, a 44-year-old Filipino, was reported. Although it was not reported at the time it occurred, it is believed that the first COVID-19 death in the United States was on February 6.

By this time, Mayor Nirenberg and I were really frustrated with the CDC, Department of Defense, and HHS for not responding to our requests to keep evacuees on base. Then they made a mistake that really shook our citizens up and permanently changed the urgency with which we would respond to the emergency.

On February 29 the CDC mistakenly released a patient from Lackland Air Force Base that had tested positive after two negative tests. She stayed at a Holiday Inn and then shopped along with hundreds of people at North Star Mall. There was a possibility she could have spread the virus, although health officials thought it was a low risk.

After it was revealed that the evacuee had tested positive, the mall closed for 24 hours and sanitized all their shops and fixtures. The incident was widely publicized. Nirenberg announced that local health officials were working very hard to prevent the spread of the virus in San Antonio and we simply could not have a screw-up like this from our federal partners.

Both Nirenberg and I have the authority to issue emergency declarations when facing a natural disaster, a public health threat, or a possible terrorist attack. Nirenberg's orders apply to the city of San Antonio; mine apply to all the two million citizens of Bexar County, which includes the city of San Antonio and 26 suburban cities and unincorporated areas. It was important that our order be consistent with each other so as not to cause conflicts and confusion.

Larry Roberson, the head of the civil section in the Bexar County District Attorney's office, prepared my emergency orders, and City Attorney Andy Segovia prepared Nirenberg's orders. The two lawyers worked together to make sure we were in sync. The emergency orders were prepared with consultation with Metro Health, UHS, and UT Health.

We were fed up with the cavalier manner that the federal government was handling the evacuees, particularly the mistake of the CDC in releasing the COVID-19 patient. As we began work on an emergency order to prevent the evacuees from entering our city, we had no idea how dangerous COVID-19 would become. We did not realize that we were about to enter a long-protracted battle against an armed-up coronavirus. COVID-19 would spread fast and harm and kill millions of people worldwide.

2. Blunting The First Attack

AT A PRESS CONFERENCE HELD IN PLAZA DE ARMAS on March 2, 2020, Mayor Nirenberg and I announced a local state of disaster and a public health emergency to preserve and protect the health of the residents of San Antonio and Bexar County. The declaration stated that no quarantined person shall be permitted to travel within the city and county. On that same day I had an interview with CNN's Erin Burnett to explain our emergency order and recent events.

The city also filed a lawsuit in federal court to force the CDC and other agencies to observe testing standards before releasing evacuees from mandatory quarantine. While the judge agreed with the concerns, the lawsuit was dismissed.

As a result of our declaration, the CDC changed their protocol for releasing those in quarantine at Lackland Air Force Base. Those that met the criteria for release were transferred on a special bus and taken directly to the airport where they were met with an airport official who escorted them to their plane.

On March 3 the evacuees from the *Diamond Princess* were bussed to the airport. However, 12 days later more passengers from the *Diamond Princess* arrived at the base.

While we focused on trying to stop the spread of COVID-19, we were hampered by the slow roll out of testing kits. The U.S. Food and Drug Administration (FDA) was a problem because they delayed giving approval to the CDC for the test.

Even after FDA approval, the CDC announced that they did not know when the testing kits would be available. They simply did not have the capacity to produce enough of them. Finally on February 29, other labs were allowed to produce kits with their own FDA-approved tests.

As we prepared to face a possible outbreak of COVID-19, the Bexar County Commissioners Court had to prepare for an important presidential election year. Additionally, two out of five Commissioners Court seats were also up for grabs. On March 3 our Bexar County Election Department, under the leadership of Election Administrator Jacque Callanen, held the Democrat and Republican primaries.

My son, Commissioner Kevin Wolff, the only Republican on the court, had decided to not seek re-election. Prior to serving 13 years on the court, he had served in the Navy and saw action while on the USS *Mahan*, a guided missile destroyer, when they participated in the battle against Muammar Gaddafi's Libya in the Gulf of Sidra on March 24, 1986.

As a county commissioner he had taken the lead to hire a county manager, the first in Texas; opened a new Veteran's Office and increased the staff; chaired the Alamo Area Council of Governments and the Metropolitan Planning Agency. He also took the lead on all county transportation projects, securing $1 billion in state funding for highway projects.

Trish DeBerry was running in the Republican primary to succeed him. DeBerry owned a public relations firm and I had worked with her on two previous bond campaigns. She was thrown into a run-off against my former opponent in the previous general election who was looking for another way to get on the Commissioners Court. In the Democrat primary, incumbent Commissioner Sergio "Chico" Rodriguez was facing a run-off with Rebeca Clay-Flores who had only spent a fraction of what Rodriguez spent on his campaign.

As the candidates were campaigning in the run-off election to be held on July 14, WHO finally declared COVID-19 a pandemic on March 11, some 48 days after they declared a PHEIC. The following day worldwide cases reached 134,000. COVID-19 was darting fast as light from one person to another and there was nothing stopping it.

One only had to look to Italy to see how bad things could get in our country. By the end of February, COVID-19 had spread to all regions of Italy. Two major soccer games had drawn over 70,000 fans to each match and became super spreader events for COVID-19.

On March 9 all of Italy was put in a lockdown and nearly all commercial activity was prohibited. Over television we saw images of overcrowded hospitals and the Italian health care system on the brink of collapse.

In March President Trump began putting in restrictions on international travel targeting European nations where COVID-19 was spreading its wings; many other nations followed suit. We also saw the effect of COVID-19 that had spread during the New Orleans Mardi Gras celebrations. Some 800 people became infected with COVID-19.

On March 13 President Trump declared a national emergency two days after WHO declared a pandemic. That same day we had our first confirmed local case of COVID-19 community spread.

Mayor Nirenberg and I held a press conference to announce that we had confirmed our first travel-related COVID-19 case. We announced that we were closing libraries, senior citizen centers, museums, and prohibiting large gatherings of 500 people or more. Nirenberg also stated that our largest annual event, Fiesta, would be postponed from April until November.

We encouraged everyone to keep a social distance of six feet apart, wash their hands frequently, don't touch their face, and sanitize surfaces: all lessons from the 1918 flu pandemic which killed 675,000 people in the United States.

St. Louis was the first city to act when the 1918 flu epidemic began. Along with the above health protocols, they were the first to ban public gatherings, shutdown schools, and close entertainment facilities. Their transparent communication and quick action resulted in the lowest mortality rate in the country.

Other cities, like Philadelphia, who waited too long suffered much worse as the flu spread throughout their communities. Subsequently a flu vaccine was developed and people across the country received vaccinations, causing the flu to retreat.

In addition to the initiatives that Nirenberg and I took, District Court Administrative Judge Ron Rangel and County Court at Law Administrative Judge John Longoria suspended jury trials. All San Antonio school districts, colleges, and universities extended spring break. CPS Energy announced that it would suspend energy disconnections for customers.

Many businesses canceled their proposed conventions and began to restrict business travel, hitting our hospitality industry hard. USAA, our largest employer with 19,000 employees, shifted employees to work from home. For example, 70 percent of Valero's 1,800 employees and the majority of SWBC's 1,900 employees began working from home.

The San Antonio Spurs games were canceled after the National Basketball Association (NBA) halted the basketball season on March 11. Two days after the NBA shut down, the San Antonio Football Club ceased playing after the United Soccer League (USL) shutdown their season. A month later in April, the San Antonio Missions Double-A baseball team canceled their games after the Texas League halted play. All three of the facilities they play in are city or county owned.

The Spurs and the Missions have a long history in San Antonio, and I had been involved with both teams dating back some 50 years. In 1968, I joined 10 other businessmen to create the San Antonio Sports Association. We built a baseball park on St. Mary University's campus, located on the west side, where the Missions played for 25 years. During my term as mayor, I led the effort to build this jewel of a ballpark that provided 6,500 seats close to the field of play. They continue to play in this park today.

In 1973, while I was serving in the Texas Senate, a local group of people bought the Dallas Chaparrals, a team in the American Basketball Association, and moved them to San Antonio. After two years of play in a small arena located in our convention center, they became one of four teams to join the NBA. In 1994 the Spurs moved to the new 65,000-seat Alamodome that was spearheaded by Mayor Henry Cisneros and built during my term as mayor.

Eleven years later, in 1999, County Judge Cyndi Krier convinced voters to build the Spurs a new arena. When I became county judge in 2001, I oversaw the construction and opened the arena in 2002. Since the opening of the county arena, the Spurs have won four national championships that added to the championship season while they had played in the Alamodome.

In 2015, I joined with Mayor Ivy Taylor to purchase Toyota Field stadium to provide a home for the San Antonio Football Club, a USL team. Spurs Sports and Entertainment also owns the San Antonio Football Club.

The county has over $200 million invested in the Spurs arena, and the city had some $15 million invested in the Mission ballpark. The city and county had $18 million invested in Toyota Field. It was clear we would have to work with our professional sports to provide some financial help to get through the pandemic. Nirenberg and I held a press conference on March 16, along with Governor Greg Abbott, at the joint city-county Emergency Operations Center located at Brooks City Base. Former Mayor Ed Garza and I had led a campaign in 2003 to convince voters to approve building the center on the heels of the 9/11 terrorist attacks.

Press conference with Mayor Ron Nirenberg, Governor Abbott, and Judge Wolff held on March 16, 2020, at the city-county Emergency Operations Center.

At the press conference Governor Abbott announced 57 confirmed cases of COVID-19 in Texas. He said he was making sure that all hospitals were getting PPE. He also recognized San Antonio for establishing the first COVID-19 testing site in Texas. Afterwards Nirenberg and I issued another emergency order that prohibited gatherings of 50 or more people.

At this point we were only testing people who had a doctor's note stating they had possible COVID-19 symptoms. Testing was provided at a portable location in a parking lot on the west side of San Antonio that Mayor Nirenberg had taken the lead on establishing. At the same time, Metro Health instituted contact tracing to determine where the person may have picked up COVID-19.

Two days after our press conference President Trump recommended that chloroquine and hydroxychloroquine be used to treat COVID-19. Dr. Fauci countered by saying it was not a promising treatment. Nevertheless Trump ordered the FDA to fast-track approval of his recommendation. Under pressure from Trump, the FDA approved emergency use. This information spread all over social media, and people started running to their doctors to be prescribed the medicine.

Three months later the FDA reversed their approval, stating that chloroquine and hydroxychloroquine were ineffective. They also reported serious cardiac adverse effects and other side effects such as kidney injury and liver problems.

After his advice did not play out too well, Trump suggested taking bleach as a disinfectant for COVID-19. He suggested that there might be a way we can use it by injection. Interesting theory. The thought entered my mind that maybe it would work better if he had suggested using chocolate flavored Tide PODS® to go along with the bleach. The pods were the rage of young people challenging each other to eat them during 2018. If we are going to get crazy, why not real crazy. While Trump's supporters lined up to get chloroquine and hydroxychloroquine, I did not notice bleach sales going up.

On the same day Trump was prescribing chloroquine and hydroxychloroquine, we opened a large COVID-19 testing site in the Bexar County Exposition Hall. We had recently built the Expo Hall on the 184-acre site where the county's coliseum and arena are located.

We developed four drive-thru testing lines to test those who had symptoms and a doctor's prescription. The San Antonio Fire Department and Metro Health ran the operation, and we were now able to test a lot more people, averaging 565 tests a day.

Nirenberg and I visited the site on the day it opened. We watched cars pull up to the Expo Hall where people had to check in and fill out forms for a polymerase chain reaction (PCR) test. PCR is a molecular test that analyzes your upper respiratory specimen looking for COVID-19. Since it was approved in February it would become the gold standard for COVID-19 tests. It was accurate and reliable.

After they checked-in, people then drove their cars to one of two tent structures that we had erected in the Expo Hall. There our health workers inserted a swab in their nose to collect material. After collecting, the swab was sealed in a tube and delivered to a collection point in the Expo Hall, where they were held until they were sent to a lab for analysis. Once Metro Health received the results from the lab, they then notified the person to tell them whether they were positive or negative.

As we would continue to expand COVID-19 testing, President Trump was saying to slow testing down. He did not want to hear about the large number of people contacting COVID-19. Of course he was wrong because testing was essential to identifying infected persons and then isolating them for 14 days, as well as the people they were in contact with.

There was another type of test used by doctors and health care providers. The antigen test detects bits of proteins (antigens) on the surface of a virus. It is a faster test, but not as accurate as PCR, especially for people without symptoms.

March 18 was a busy day as I also presented to the Commissioners Court a proposal to activate our own public health advisors. While we would continue our relationship with Metro Health, we wanted another set of expert eyes and ears we could turn to for guidance.

We brought on Dr. Ruth Berggren, director of UT Health's Center for Medical Humanities and Ethics. She had received her medical degree from Harvard University. She was certified in internal medicine and had previously worked on viruses and vaccines. Dr. Bryan Alsip, medical director for the Bexar County Hospital District, and Seth Mitchell, my former chief of staff, joined our team. Our team would advise me on the emergency orders that I would issue as well as advise the Commissioners Court on necessary health and safety issues we should take. Bexar County Public Information Officer Monica Ramos was responsible for explaining to the public the decisions we would make.

In addition to creating our Bexar County team, the Commissioners Court appropriated five million dollars in loans and grants for small businesses to assist them during the pandemic.

The following day on March 19, Governor Abbott issued an emergency order to limit social gatherings to no more than 10 people, and close restaurant dining areas and all bars. Closing restaurants got my attention because he went further than my previous order requiring spacing and sanitizing for restaurants.

Governor Abbott's order made me the odd man out since Mayor Nirenberg had issued his order to close restaurant dining rooms and bars the day before. I needed to get on the same page and not cause confusion with our citizens, so I adjusted my emergency order to conform to the mayor and governor. My order went further and prevented any price increases for groceries, beverages, toilet articles, medicine, and meals, as well as suspending evictions and foreclosures.

At the same time, Texas Health and Human Services Commissioner Dr. John Hellerstedt declared a public health disaster, the first in over 100 years. He called COVID-19 the greatest health challenge in living memory.

I had a WebEx meeting with all the mayors of the 26 suburban cities in Bexar County on March 20 to bring them up to date on COVID-19. Previously we had quarterly in-person meetings to discuss local, state, and national issues. Throughout the pandemic we would continue to meet over WebEx and Zoom.

A woman in her 80s became our first fatal COVID-19 case in Bexar County on March 21. The following day Nirenberg and I huddled with health experts and lawyers to develop an emergency order that would in effect shut down most of our economy. Our previous order closing restaurant dining rooms was small potatoes compared to what we were now discussing. My stomach churned as I thought about the jobs that would be lost and the businesses that would fail.

I had spent most of my life in business as a co-founder and operator of two companies. In 1961 my dad and I, along with my two brothers, founded Alamo Enterprises that grew into an eight-store chain of building material stores. We sold to it to Evans Corporation in 1977. In 1987 my two brothers and I, along with our friends Don and Ron Hermann, founded Sun Harvest Natural Food supermarket, that grew into a nine-store chain. We sold it to Wild Oats in 1999, a national chain of 100 stores.

So, I knew how difficult it was to compete against the big boys when operating a small business. And now small businesses would be faced with a shut down that would threaten their ability to survive.

While I had great concerns about a shut down, I know we had to move forward because our hospitals were not ready for an influx of COVID-19 patients. If hospitals were stretched beyond their capacity, it would affect anybody seeking medical help for any serious sickness or injury.

The hospitals needed time to staff up and buy PPE such as gloves, gowns, and N95 masks. They had to be able to separate COVID-19 patients from other patients, install negative air flow to COVID-19 patient rooms, and create other safety measures.

Our hospital problems were compounded by the Trump administration's failure to organize a federal approach to acquiring PPE. The Trump administration left it up to the 50 governors to acquire PPE. A mad scramble unfolded as each governor sought to buy PPE, resulting in bidding wars. It would take some time to provide all Texas hospitals with protective equipment.

It was a hard pill for me to swallow, but it was clear that we had to act quickly and decisively to protect our city from a surge of COVID-19 cases that would overwhelm our hospitals. We had seen that happen in European cities.

We continued work on Monday, March 23, and by late afternoon we issued an extraordinary emergency order. We named it "Stay Home, Work Safe." It directed non-essential businesses to close and directed residents to remain in their homes, with the exception of crucial errands and job duties. Working safe at home and closing non-essential businesses would stop a spike of COVID-19 and flatten the curve.

We were one of the first cities and counties, if not the first, in the United States to issue an order that virtually shut the city down. Rather than a city or county taking such an action, states had begun to do so a few days earlier. According to Timeanddate. com, California and Nevada issued a similar order to ours on the 19th and 20th, followed by the states of Illinois and New Jersey on March 21. Louisiana and New York acted the day before our order. At the time we issued our order Texas had not issued a stay-at-home order.

While no one could leave home unless it was essential to do so, we knew that the internet and advanced technology allowed many to work from home. Several businesses had already implemented the technology to allow employees to work from home.

Bexar County Chief Information Officer Mark Gager was quick to react to develop the technology to allow all of our employees to work from home. Within one week employees whose jobs enabled them to work from home were provided the laptops and connections to work from home.

Our emergency order did keep essential businesses open. We drew our list from the U.S. Department of Homeland Security's guidance. Businesses such as health care, manufacturing, construction, and essential government services stayed open.

Based on the Texas Department of Emergency Management's recommendations, we also kept businesses open that sold essential products to customers, such as grocery stores, building material stores, and plumbing and electrical services. Governor Abbott stated the day after our emergency order, "Local officials have the authority to implement more strict standards than I as governor have implemented in the state of Texas."

Not everybody was buying into the shutdown. On March 24, Lieutenant Governor Dan Patrick announced that he and other grandparents would be willing to risk their health and even their lives in order for the United States to get back to work. But sacrificing the elderly, who are the most vulnerable to dying from COVID-19, was not an option that Mayor Nirenberg and I would consider. Nirenberg told CNN, "I am not willing to sacrifice any one of my residents, let alone those workers on the front lines of this battle, the health care workers, or the 100,000 plus veterans in this community who are older Americans who have served this country. It's time to we step up and serve them."

We soon found out that COVID-19 patients would spend more time in the hospital than expected, making less room available for other patients. For example, if you had the flu, the median length of stay in the hospital was 3.6 days, in contrast to a COVID-19 patient who would stay an average of 10 days. If a COVID-19 patient was in the ICU, the stay was up to 10 days and 11 days on a ventilator.

It was disheartening to see how the Trump administration was not prepared for the pandemic and downplayed it as it evolved. The Obama administration had developed a 69-page playbook for early response to high consequence emerging infectious disease threats and biological incidents. At the top of list were respiratory viruses. The Trump administration had disregarded the report and dismantled the pandemic response team created by President Obama.

***

As I thought about the strong actions Nirenberg and I were taking to protect our citizens and the confusing messages that President Trump was sending out, I wondered if the COVID-19 crisis would split our nation rather than unite it as President George Bush did when the 9/11 terrorist attacks occurred.

It began on the morning of Tuesday, September 11, 2001, when Tracy shouted at me as I came into the house from my daily run, "Quick, come in here and watch this." I rushed into our bedroom to see the top floors of the North and South Towers of the World Trade Center aflame and smoking. An airplane had hit the North Tower, and another had hit the South Tower. I quickly showered, dressed, and headed for the courthouse. As I drove to the courthouse, I listened to the events unfold over public radio.

By the time I convened the Commissioners Court at 9:30 a.m., both the South and the North Towers had collapsed. We then learned that another plane had crashed into the Pentagon and yet another in the countryside of Pennsylvania.

I quickly adjourned the meeting and signed an emergency order that included expanded criminal intelligence operations, increased security, surveillance of public facilities, law enforcement and fire personnel on heightened alter status, and all non-essential county personnel released at noon. Mayor Ed Garza closed the airport. At the time these were extraordinary actions to take that would have long-term effects on our society.

Two months after the attack, Tracy and I traveled to New York over the Thanksgiving weekend. We first visited with my son, Kevin, who was living there at the time with his wife, Sandi, and their daughter, Sydney, in their condo on 94th Street. Kevin and I took a subway to the New York City Office of Emergency Management located at Pier 92 off 55th street.

We met with Deputy Director Robert Rotanz who gave us a thorough briefing, and then we went to the World Trade Center site with Captain Thomas DePrisco. We stood on a large wooden platform and looked down on the 16-acre site at the skeletons of three buildings and several buildings on the periphery that were damaged. Looking at the haunting view of burnt steel and rubble I knew our country's surveillance and security would be increased, possibility leading to threats to our liberty.

Nelson Wolff and Captain Thomas DePrisco on platform viewing ground zero.

I used the information I gathered in New York to develop an anti-terrorism plan. District Attorney Susan Reed and I consulted with over 200 jurisdictions and emergency response organizations. The plan provided for the creation of a redundant backup and enhanced communication system. Additional training, equipment, and investigative capabilities were delineated. It called for the combining of the city and county emergency operations and the building of a new emergency operations center. After implementing these changes, a CNN report ranked San Antonio second in the nation among the 30 largest cities in terms of emergency readiness.

We united as a nation under President Bush's leadership and accepted the change in our society as we moved toward a more secure environment. After the terrorist attack, an overhaul and expansion of government intelligence services were instituted as well as the creation of new agencies such as the United States Department of Homeland Security.

The Transportation Security Administration was also created that provided airport security by screening passengers and periodic searches of carry-ons. The private sector, as well as government agencies, also increased security on their buildings, with many requiring scanning. The government compiled more information about all of us through intelligence gathering.

President Bush relied on the advice of experts as he implemented the above measures. As a result, he united our nation as we accepted increased security. President Trump chose to ignore safety protocols that were recommended by medical experts and unfortunately led us into a swirling cyclone. Unfortunately, President Trump preferred to divide and conquer rather than inspire and unite. It seemed inevitable from early misleading statements that he would approach the COVID-19 epidemic as he had other issues—in a state of chaos.

In a *Washington Post* interview, Nirenberg said, "Throughout the course of this, what I've seen is that the lack of coordination at the highest levels of the president's administration is simply stunning."

Over time President Trump would disregard expert advice, resort to blistering personal attacks, and lead us into a fractured nation. He was not one to join hands.

While President Trump would resort to divisiveness, Nirenberg and I were in sync with Texas Republican Governor Abbott. Bipartisan leadership was important in creating clear messages to the public. Governor Abbott had supported our local efforts to protect our citizens such as our "Stay Home, Work Safe" mandate. But time would eventually tell us a different story about Abbott's bipartisan leadership.

***

While "Stay Home, Work Safe" was protecting our citizens from COVID-19, our economy was taking a big hit and many businesses were suffering. In the short term there would be serious consequences to many businesses. Jobs would be lost, and many businesses would fail. That is why the Commissioners Court was first to step up and offer five million dollars in loans and grants to small businesses. The federal government would have to step in and provide substantial relief for the overall economy.

I must tell you that I had a sick, scary feeling as I drove down the traffic-free streets to the courthouse. San Antonio was like a ghost town, particularly downtown. Tourism is a significant part of our economy, and our downtown hotels were virtually empty. When I arrived at the courthouse very few souls were around as all court proceedings had been canceled.

What few buses I saw were virtually empty. Public transportation was discouraged because of the proximity of people in a closed environment. But our public transit authority, VIA, under the leadership of President Jeff Arndt, kept operating by keeping passengers spaced out and requiring them to wear face masks. People with limited income had no choice but public transit, and Nirenberg and I both supported VIA's decision.

The "Stay Home, Work Safe" order had a major impact on families and individuals. Remote working at home allowed parents to be at home with their young children, saving on childcare, commuting cost, and food cost. Most families flourished, connecting with each other and spending more time together.

But there was also a bad side. Some of those who lived alone struggled with mental health problems in their isolation. Local kennels experienced a run of people wanting to adopt a dog for a companion.

Under the leadership of President Jelynne LeBlanc Burley, Bexar County Center for Health Care Services set up a special line to call for any emergency mental health crises, including those who may harm themselves and refuse to take treatment. For those who refused treatment a mental health warrant was issued.

Domestic violence also increased causing the Commissioners Court to fund three additional assistant district attorneys to handle requests for protective orders.

COVID-19 would cause an adjustment for my wife Tracy and myself. This was the first time in 33 years of marriage that we were both working from home.

Tracy is totally a germ fighter, even to the extent of making me take off my clothes in the garage before I came into the house. She would also spray my shoes with disinfectant. The shoes and clothes would stay in the garage for at least three hours, long enough to decontaminate. Walking into your home in your underwear is a weird feeling.

At home I was constantly on the phone or using video conferencing. My administrative assistant Anna Marie Ruiz adjusted to scheduling conference calls rather than in-person meetings. I had not heard of Zoom or WebEx, so my communication director James Rivera became my personal tech-support guy, teaching me all the fundamentals. I soon learned all the technical issues, and over time began to relish it. It saved a great deal of time not having to rush to so many in-person meetings.

One of the most vexing issues that Tracy and I faced was not being able to see our two youngest grandchildren, Gideon, age four, and Madeline, age two. My son Matthew and his wife Molly, a registered nurse, were very protective of their children—thank goodness. We were not allowed to visit in person, and rightly so. We had to rely on Zoom to visit with them.

I continued my daily two-mile jog, although at age 79 I was a lot slower, taking about 30 minutes. I learned to take three deep breaths through my nose in order for air to go directly to my lungs. I found it invigorating while at the same time I was conscious about my breathing capacity, fearful COVID-19 might shut me down.

I was appointed by Tracy to gather food and found myself standing in line outside the Alon H-E-B grocery store. Staff was on hand to encourage people to wear masks and remain six feet apart. When I entered and walked down the aisles, I passed by shelves empty of disinfectants, sanitizing products, and toilet paper. Some food products were missing, but not many because the store had put purchase limits on food products like eggs, bread, and milk. People continued to hoard certain products such as toilet paper. I thought that was so strange. Grocery store leaders tried to assure customers that there was no need to hoard as supply chains were working.

Many people began to grow their own vegetables but also found shortages when they could not find seeds. Our county manager David Smith created a garden of potatoes, tomatoes, and squash, but it was smaller than he planned because he couldn't find enough seeds or small starter plants. Some people began buying chickens for their egg supply, but soon found only a few chicks were available.

Even though COVID-19 was spreading and causing death, some people continued to downplay the pandemic, saying it was no different than the annual flu that we face. While some symptoms were similar—fever, cough, and fatigue—COVID-19 also caused shortness of breath, headaches, sore throat, stuffy nose, body aches, and oddly, the loss of taste and smell. Flu was contagious for three to five days after infection, but COVID-19 lasted much longer.

During the 2002-03 SAR-COV epidemic only people with symptoms could spread the disease. Dr. Fauci had said it would be unusual for asymptomatic persons to drive an epidemic, but the unusual was here. COVID-19 had a new powerful weapon that would accelerate the spread. The CDC had delayed for two months before it acknowledged that asymptomatic people could spread COVID-19. It now encouraged testing of asymptomatic people.

On March 25 Trump issued a major disaster declaration for Texas, opening up new federal funding resources for the state. On that same day the last of the evacuees from the *Diamond Princess* cruise ship were released from their two-week, federally mandated quarantine at Joint Base San Antonio-Lackland.

The following day we began a daily conference call that included City Manager Erik Walsh, Assistant City Manager Dr. Colleen Bridger who oversaw Metro Health, Metro Health Director Dawn Emerick, County Manager David Smith, Fire Chief Charles Hood, STRAC Director Eric Epley, Nirenberg's Communication Director Bruce Davidson, Bexar County Public Information Officer Monica Ramos, my Chief of Staff Nicole Erfurth, Nirenberg, and me. From time-to-time others would join us on the call.

As we talked, we each had a Daily Situation Report before us prepared by city staff and the Bexar County Office of Emergency Management. Fire Chief Hood would go over the number of hospital transports and testing results. STRAC Director Eric Epley gave us the number of people in hospital including a breakout for ICU and those on ventilators, and most importantly how many staffed beds and ventilators were available. Metro Health staff would review the new COVID-19 cases, nursing-home outbreaks, the number of deaths, and how many were tested that day.

We would then discuss the report and decide what action we should take, whether it would be a new emergency order or a change in health guidelines. The report would become the basis of the daily media briefing session that Nirenberg and I would begin March 27.

The following day at the invitation of all the local television stations Mayor Nirenberg and I started hosting a live broadcast at 6:13 p.m. We held the media briefing in a first-class studio that the city had set up in the historic Plaza de Armas building located next to the Spanish Governor's Palace and 100 feet or so behind the historic city hall.

My security team, consisting of Deputy Joe Quiroz and Juan Guillen, would alternate on picking me up. We usually arrived about 5:45 p.m. at Plaza de Armas. My chief of staff Nicole Erfurth would join me in the car as we went over the script for Mayor Nirenberg that had been prepared by city staff. The mayor's script would be a compilation of the information from the daily situation report.

Nicole and I then would go over the notes that she and I had both prepared from reading up-to-date information from different sources regarding COVID-19. I wanted to speak directly to people, giving them the best advice from the information we had accumulated. After Nirenberg gave highlights from the report, I would then provide my commentary. Then we would take questions from members of the media who attended, as well questions submitted through Bruce Davidson. We usually had someone from Metro Health on the show to answer the more technical questions.

Judge Nelson Wolff and Mayor Nirenberg talking before one of the media briefing sessions.

In our first media briefing on March 27, Nirenberg stated that our community had 120 confirmed cases of COVID-19, five deaths, and 33 in the hospital. He went over the need to wear face coverings, social distance, and not meet in large groups.

I spoke about the need to sanitize surfaces, advising people how COVID-19 will eventually decay, but the timing was different depending on the surface and on the temperature and humidity. I pointed out that on clothes COVID-19 could last up to three hours (the reason for Tracy's requirement to disrobe before entering our home). COVID-19 would last on wood for four hours, cardboard 24 hours, metal 42 hours, and plastic 72 hours. I pointed out that COVID-19 is stable in moisture so dehumidify rooms and stay in a dry, bright environment. Washing hands with soap and hot water would destroy COVID-19.

On the same day of the first show, President Trump signed an unprecedented $2.2 trillion economic rescue plan called Coronavirus Aid, Relief, and Economic Security Act (CARES). It included financial support for small businesses, payroll protection to save jobs, and rent assistance.

Later, Bexar County received a check for $79,626,415.00 and the city of San Antonio received $270,000,000.00 from the CARES act funding. The City Council and the Commissioners Court then made the decisions of how to allocate the funds under the guidelines of the CARES Act.

Three days later Nirenberg and I announced that we were creating five community action committees to address state and federal advocacy, philanthropy, food security and shelter, business and employment, and social services and health transition.

The following day we announced that we would open a 250-bed field hospital at the Bexar County Expo Hall to handle any overload that our hospital might face. By this point we had 52 patients in the hospital of which 21 were in intensive care.

While we struggled with containing the virus, the only answer to COVID-19 would be the development of a vaccine. And that would take time as no vaccine for the coronavirus family had ever been developed.

HHS started a program called "Operation Warp Speed" on

March 30. A huge amount of federal dollars was allocated to pharmaceutical and biotechnology firms to conduct large-scale clinical trials for new vaccines that would be developed. They also allocated funds for the purchase of the vaccines once they were developed.

I had my doubts about whether a vaccine would ever be developed. I had seen the failure to develop a vaccine during the deadliest pandemic we had faced in modern times.

As a first term councilman in 1987, my friend Hap Veltman came to visit me. Veltman had been a major player in the development of the downtown river walk and the Blue Star Arts complex that included a contemporary museum, art studios, and apartments. He walked in my office with a cane holding up his emaciated body. He asked for help from local government for those who had been infected with HIV, the human immunodeficiency virus. He was one of them.

Identified in 1984, the HIV infection spread across the world, caused by body fluids exchanged primarily through unprotected anal or vaginal sex as well as through needle sharing. The chronic infection is because the virus incorporates itself into our own DNA, becoming latent, and our immune system cannot kill latent viruses. The virus kills immune T helper cells that are coordinators of the human immune system. It was a sure death sentence in its early stages.

After being identified in 1984, HHS Secretary Margaret Heckler stated that she hoped to have a vaccine ready for testing in about two years. How wrong she would be.

When I became mayor seven years later in 1991, there was still no HIV vaccine available. We began funding numerous programs to help those who were infected. My wife Tracy began working with Papa Bear, a bar owner, who had taken on the responsibility to provide a safe place for those who were in the last stages of the disease.

When I became County Judge in 2001 there still was no vaccine. As County Judge I was responsible for administering federal HIV/AIDS grants to help educate people about safe sex, needle exchange programs, and treating people with AIDS.

Finally in 2009 the results of the largest HIV vaccine trial were announced. It was partially successful, attaining a 31 percent level of efficacy but not high enough to warrant the use of a vaccine. But there was hope as work continued.

While we still do not have a vaccine for HIV, antiretroviral treatment has extended life to near normal and reduced the transmission of the virus significantly. Medical advisor to the president Dr. Antony Fauci has played a major role in the antiretroviral treatment. In 2008 President George W. Bush awarded him the Presidential Medal of Freedom for his work on AIDS. By 2019 some 38 million were still living with HIV/AIDS, yet 690,000 deaths occurred in the same year. Over 32 million people have died since HIV/AIDS was identified in 1984.

While I was leery of the quick success in developing a COVID-19 vaccine, I was hopeful and thankful for the federal response. At least the proposed vaccine would not be faced with the same hurdles that HIV/AIDS presented. The variability of HIV types and lack of a natural immunity to HIV were huge obstacles to overcome.

At the same time as we were turning to the pharmaceutical industry for help on COVID-19, Bexar County was in a lawsuit against many of the firms claiming false and misleading advertising related to the distribution of opioids.

The proliferation of legal addictive drugs, such as Oxy-

Contin®, led to thousands of people becoming addicted and many of them dying from overdose. The COVID-19 pandemic would make matters even worse. Lockdowns, isolation, evictions, loss of job, and other factors had led to mental stress and higher use of opioid drugs, both legal and illegal.

While the COVID-19 vaccine development continued, our job was to concentrate on health safety measures. On April 1, Nirenberg and I sent a letter to our faith community requesting that all religious worship and prayer services continue to be conducted through remote services. We were aware of what happened near Seattle, Washington, at a choir practice on March 10. Out of 61 singers, 53 tested positive and two passed away. Singing in church, or for that matter anywhere, releases aerosols than can easily spread.

On April 1, 2020, I wrote a memo to the Commissioner's Court about FDA alerts regarding fraudulent COVID-19 tests. Many different companies were marketing tests that were not FDA approved. The FDA stated that they had not approved home testing and warned that fraudulent tests could pose serious health risks.

I wrote the memo to the commissioners because one company was trying to sell the county unauthorized FDA tests. This company had convinced two of our commissioners to use an unauthorized home test. Finally, the company backed off and I believe eventually went out of business.

On the same day, we had an outbreak of COVID-19 at the Southeast nursing home located on Southcross Street. Elderly people with underlying health issues are very vulnerable, especially those clustered together in a cohort. Mayor Nirenberg and I issued additional emergency orders that strengthened controls on nursing homes including no visitors, no transferring of personnel from one nursing home to another, and requiring testing and separating out patients with symptoms.

Throughout the pandemic we monitored each nursing home through numerous inspections to see if they were complying with health protocols. In our daily situation reports we kept a list of any nursing home who had COVID-19 cases and targeted the worst offenders with increased inspections.

On April 2, eight days after we issued our "Stay Home, Work Safe" order, Governor Abbott announced a state-wide emergency order closing down all businesses except for essential businesses. He largely followed the emergency order that Nirenberg and I had implemented. He also named a strike force to make recommendations on how and when to open up Texas in a safe manner.

The following day after Abbott's order, we finally had enough COVID-19 test kits available to offer testing to those with symptoms, but we still required a doctor's certificate. It would take time to gear up to test asymptomatic people.

One of the issues that perplexed us was why the CDC announced that only people who were sick or caring for someone who was sick should wear a face covering. With COVID-19 spreading we were not buying that. We thought everyone should wear a mask when they were within close proximity to another person. I began wearing a bandana and Nirenberg a face mask.

People watching our media briefing became enamored with my bandana—I guess because I looked like an outlaw. They started sending me special designed bandanas and I would wear them on the show and thank them. I ended up with 25 different bandanas. Later I would I wear a mask as studies showed the bandana was not as effective. But I still wore them as a necktie during our briefings.

It did not take the CDC long to wake up and reverse their guideline on masks. On April 3 they said they recommended face coverings for everyone, whether they had symptoms or not. It was recognition that asymptomatic people were becoming significant spreaders of COVID-19.

Throughout the early stages of the COVID-19 pandemic the CDC had been slow to act. First saying the pandemic was a low risk, then stumbling on test kits, and finally not recognizing that asymptomatic people could spread COVID-19. I believe you can trace back their hesitancy to the 1976 outbreak of swine flu (H1N1). Early on David Sencer, Director of the CDC, decided to take aggressive action while facing scientific uncertainty about the severity of swine flu.

He invoked the precautionary principle that states if a proposed event is low probability, but high impact, then you should respond aggressively. He quickly launched a massive vaccination program. He was quoted as saying, "When lives are at stake, it is better to err on the side of overreaction than underreaction."

Unfortunately, Guillain-Barre syndrome, a disorder that can cause paralysis, respiratory arrest, and death, was found in some cases stemming from the vaccinations. According to the CDC, of the 45 million vaccinated people, 450 developed the rare disorder; that is one out of every 100,000 people. The exact reason remains unknown to this day as to why there was an association between the vaccine and this terrible disorder.

Even though only 25 percent were vaccinated, there was no major outbreak of the new strain of flu. Secretary of Health and Welfare Joseph A. Califano, Jr. fired Sencer. I believe that the leadership at the CDC never forgot the incident, and as a result they became cautious when facing the virus outbreak.

On our April 10 media briefing, I announced that our first Bexar County jail inmate had tested positive as well as 12 employees of the sheriff. We had required inmates and jail guards to wear masks, and every day we cleaned and sanitized cells. But these measures would eventually prove to be inadequate. Our numbers continued to go up each day among our 3,500–4,000 inmates. This was unacceptable.

Under the guidance of our county health team, led by Dr. Ruth Berggren and Seth Mitchell, they assembled a team of county and UHS officials to a conference call to develop health strategies for the jail. The final plan included separation and isolation, jail space repurposing, temperature tests, COVID-19 tests, and limited inmate movement.

After the plan was adopted, Mitchell was initially frustrated that they were not getting the response from emergency management that they needed. While cohort settings such as nursing homes were targeted and everyone was tested, our jail was the largest congregate facility in the city, and comprehensive testing was not implemented.

Finally, COVID-19 tests were given to every inmate that came into the jail. It was a major undertaking as approximately 100 new inmates enter the jail every day. Approximately 550 workers commute to and from the jail each day, raising the risk of exposing people outside the jail's walls.

We were fortunate that the Commissioners Court had funded the building of a new five-story facility with 864 beds to take the place of decommissioned jail beds. The large first floor provided space where the arrested person could be tested for COVID-19 and have an initial screening process to reveal any mental health problems. UHS personnel were on hand to provide services for any arrestee who had health complications.

Those that tested positive were put in the COVID-19 unit and all others were held in separate cell blocks for 14 days (the incubation period). The space could hold up to 300 arrested people.

We had also opened a new infirmary in the South Tower holding 64 beds and the East Tower with 48 beds. We began to dramatically bring down our COVID-19 cases in the jail. From a high of 326 positive inmates on May 15, the numbers began to rapidly turn downward to the point where we reached single digits. The testing worked as inmates were separated according to the testing results.

While we were taking strong protective measures to contain COVID-19, Governor Abbott also provided leadership. He ordered the Texas Parks and Wildlife Department and the Texas Historical Commission to temporarily close all state parks and historical sites. This was another responsible step by the governor. By the middle of April, the economic toll began to hit home. Our unemployed rose from about 3 percent pre-COVID-19 to 12 percent. The pandemic hit the lowest band of our economy the hardest. Hotel clerks, maids, waiters, retail clerks, and many others in the service industry lost their jobs.

While we continued our fight against COVID-19, we reached out to help people who were facing financial difficulties. We prohibited evictions, gave rent and utility subsidies, and instituted other programs to help. For example, San Antonio Food Bank President Eric Cooper, hosted a mega food distribution at Trader's Village, a large outdoor market space. Mayor Nirenberg joined volunteers as they handed out more than one million pounds of food to 6,000 families.

Our tourism industry had taken a huge hit. The hotel/motel taxes had collapsed leading to a $100 million shortfall for the city. The city had to furlough 270 municipal employees. At the same time our entertainment venues took a huge hit.

On April 17, Governor Abbott issued an emergency order to postpone all surgeries/procedures that were not medically necessary. Hospitals had to certify to the HHS Commissioner that they would reserve at least 25 percent of hospital capacity for the treatment of COVID-19 patients.

The governor also closed Texas public schools for in person learning for the remainder of the school year. Prior to the school closing announcement, I had talked with Northside Independent School District (NISD) Superintendent Brian Woods several times. NISD is the fourth largest school district in the state of Texas and the largest in Bexar County with 105,000 students.

Woods told me he was conflicted. He was worried about the detrimental education effects on children as well as the hardship on families. He wondered whether children were any safer with schools closed because in many cases both parents had to work and send their children to childcare centers.

Putting his doubts aside, Woods had been working with his technology, curriculum, and instruction teams since March 6. He informed teachers they had a few days to prepare lessons that could be taught online. He then organized a call of the Bexar County's 15 superintendents on March 14 to discuss actions they could work on together. All the superintendents agreed to move online, even though their technology structure was not ready for full implementation.

After being granted authority in an emergency meeting with his board of trustees, Woods moved forward to purchase the technology equipment he needed, compensate his employees, and deal with leave issues. They patched together what they could for online learning and began online classes in earnest the week of March 23.

As Woods prepared for online learning, he also had to deal with demand for take-away meals for students. He said in many cases, lines were hundreds of cars deep. He thought that demand was based mostly on fear generated by tight supplies of food in grocery stores and named a "Food Czar" to handle the crisis. Since then, NISD delivered millions of pounds of food out of their cafeterias in cooperation with the San Antonio Food Bank.

On the same day that Abbott shut down schools Mayor Nirenberg and I issued an emergency order requiring everyone over 10 years old to wear a face covering. A fine up to $1,000 or up to six months in jail was imposed for failure to wear one. This was not a popular order as resistance arose from those claiming that we were stepping on individual freedoms. The jail term was particularly irritating and would later lead to political storm.

Shelly Luther, the owner of Salon A la Mode in Dallas, opened her salon on April 24 in violation of Governor Abbott's emergency order. She was sentenced to seven days in jail and a $7,000 fine under a local emergency order.

With his back to the wall and facing a hot curling iron, three days later Governor Abbott issued Executive Order GA-22 stating that no jurisdiction would be allowed to confine anyone to jail for violating any order issued in response to the COVID-19 disaster.

I thought the governor made a good decision overruling local orders that provided for jail terms. We made a mistake including a jail term in our emergency orders. Sending someone to jail for a violation would only make them a hero—as it did when Luther used her notoriety to run for the Texas Senate but lost.

***

On April 27 Mayor Nirenberg and I took a tour of the Battelle Mask Decontamination site located in the Bexar County Exposition Hall. We passed by several huge oven-looking metal containers filled with concentrated hydrogen peroxide vapor used to destroy bacteria, viruses, and contaminants. Because of the shortage of PPE, the system could clean the same N95 mask up to 20 times.

The site would remain open until September 2020. I believe the reason they closed was because most hospitals had their own decontamination processes. I thought it was a lot of wasted federal money.

By the end of April our emergency "Stay Home, Work Safe" order, along with health safety protocols including a face covering mandate, had prevented our hospitals from becoming overloaded with COVID-19 patients. That gave us time to open more COVID-19 beds, staff them properly, and purchase protective equipment and clothing. This was important to COVID-19 patients as well as other patients who had serious medical conditions.

We led the large metro areas of the state with less COVID-19 cases, fewer people in the hospital, and fewer deaths. On the last day of April, we only had 55 people in the hospital with 31 in ICU and 22 on ventilators.

Dr. Juan Gutierrez, the chair of mathematics at UTSA ran a model that showed our early response had prevented an explosion in the number of cases. He said they would have been significantly higher had Nirenberg and I not acted early.

By May 1, 2020, it appeared that we had successfully blunted the spread of COVID-19. We were down to 60 COVID-19 patients in the hospital, and our daily confirmed COVID-19 cases were holding steady, even with more tests being conducted.

The strong actions of Governor Abbott along with our emergency orders had seemingly crippled Mr. COVID and allowed us to manage the pandemic without a major outbreak. But too often in war, victory seems in hand, and you disarm, only to find out you were fooled.

3. Unilateral Disarmament

On May 5, Abbott issued a new emergency order that opened up all Texas businesses except for gyms, bars, barbershops, hair and nail salons, and summer camps. He also did away with the mandatory health and safety measures. Nirenberg criticized the governor for dropping health protocols and opening businesses too fast and too soon. "We're getting there. We're not there yet," he warned.

I did not have a problem with businesses opening because we had prepared our hospitals with all the necessary protective equipment, and they were ready to accept COVID-19 patients. But I did say he had made a fatal mistake in doing away with mandatory health and safety measures that would be enforced through fines and frequent inspections.

Without the safety measures he was jeopardizing business openings by endangering their employees and customers with the spread of COVID-19. I wanted the business openings to be successful, but I seriously doubted they would be. There was no doubt in my mind that he had messed up.

I believe Abbott was going on the assumption that COVID-19 would quickly die out during the summer and that the

March-April shutdown was viewed as a bridge to June when things would get better. Maybe he was right, after all the dry heat of summer might could quash COVID-19. Maybe more people would stay outside in the summer where it is safer, but I had my doubts. The heat of summer would cause too many people to sit on their couch in their air-conditioned homes feeling comfortable but providing a nice environment for COVID-19 to spread among family members.

After Abbott's announcement, several medical experts said that while our positive cases had dropped, they had not been proven to be sustainable. That would eventually prove true, but people were ready to get out of their homes, return to work, and go back to normal life. The governor's order was a clear signal that the coast was clear.

Many companies were cautious about bringing people back to work, allowing many of them to continue working from home. Other businesses encouraged their employees to return to work but kept safety measures in place. For example, International Bank of Commerce President Dennis Nixon and Frost Bank President Phil Green opened their lobbies but restricted occupancy.

On the same day as Governor Abbott's emergency order became effective, we had a joint City Council-County Commissioners meeting via WebEx. We heard reports from the community action working groups and the Economic Transition Team.

In a virtual community meeting, the room you are sitting in can become a worldwide discussion. I was in my home library that features a nine-foot-high wall of books, along with a table full of larger books, and two glass cases of books and antiques. A video of the meeting popped up on the Twitter account Room Rater that rates rooms and backgrounds of individuals on video calls. I ended up with 965 likes and comments including, "Does this guy live in a museum," and "His book collection is impressive."

On May 12 Attorney General Ken Paxton sent Mayor Nirenberg and me a nasty, vile letter stating that we were violating the Governor's order. He wrote, "Your local order unlawfully trampled on religious freedom. Your order conflicts with the Governor's order by attempting to impose a criminal penalty for violations. Your orders to require individuals to wear a mask when they leave home is a violation...they are free to choose whether to wear one or not. Your order that Business must provide face masks is superseded by the governor's order."

I stated on our daily media briefing that we had received a "love letter" from the attorney general and went on to criticize the inaccuracy of it as well as its tone, calling it a political stunt. Nirenberg said Paxton was seeking a cheap political headline. Both of us continued to ask citizens to practice social distancing, wear face coverings, wash their hands, and sanitize surfaces.

To underscore the tragic decision of the governor to take away our face covering mandate, a new study and computer model led by De Lai, an American computer scientist associated with UC Berkeley's International Science Institute and Hong Kong's University of Science and Technology, provided new evidence that wearing a mask, whether surgical, homemade, scarf or bandana, was the most important deterrent to COVID-19. If 80 percent of the population would wear one, infection rates would drop to approximately one twelfth of the number of infections.

Another study by University of Hong Kong led by Dr. Yuen Kwok-Young found that masks slowed the spread of COVID-19 by 75 percent. Kwok-Young is a leading microbiologist who had discovered the SARS-CoV 2002-03 now known as SARS-CoV-1.

Of course, the United States would never achieve an 80 percent mask compliance. President Trump made fun of people who wore masks, prompting a huge movement by the anti-mask crowd to discourage any mandate. Mask mandates would become a litmus test for the right wing of the Republican party who ascribed to the philosophy that freedom of choice means giving everyone the right to get COVID-19 and then infect others.

While the governor had exhibited great leadership the first three months of the pandemic, he leaned right on May 5, 2020, when he stripped us of the authority to mandate face coverings and other health safety protocols. Mr. COVID-19 noticed that Texas would prove to be an ideal hunting ground to launch a laser strike.

For the first 14 days after the implementation of the governor's order, we rose from 55 COVID-19 patients in the hospital to 80 on May 19. While Abbott did not consider our rise in hospitalization a concern, he would find out that Mr. COVID is sneaky when he starts to slip up on you. He would catch the governor with his pants down.

To prepare for the run-off election, on May 14 the Commissioners Court passed a resolution that said anyone who perceived a risk to their health because of COVID-19 could vote by mail. Attorney General Paxton ruled that fear of COVID-19 did not meet the state's definition of disability. He sent a letter stating that we could face criminal charges if we advised voters, who were fearful of COVID-19, to vote by mail. I stated that his opinion was not the law, and we should press forward.

Paxton filed a lawsuit asking the federal court to uphold his opinion. Bexar County won at the federal district court level when my longtime friend Federal Judge Fred Biery stated, "The Court finds the Grim Reaper's scepter of pandemic disease and death is far more serious than an unsupported fear of voter fraud."

Elation did not last as the U.S. Fifth Circuit Court chose to ignore the grim reaper and overruled Biery. But at the state court level the Texas Supreme Court did give us an opening by ruling that if a person declares he has a health issue that precludes him from voting in person, his decision cannot be questioned by an election administrator.

The run-off election became more difficult when Bexar County Chair of the Republican party Cynthia Brehm announced on May 23 that coronavirus was a hoax perpetuated by the Democrat party. She went on to say that this is America, and we should not be forced to wear a mask. She encouraged people to take off their masks, and she attacked the mayor and me for advocating masks. She had 18,000 likes on Twitter. The spread of crazy was moving as fast as COVID-19.

In our daily media briefing I stated that my great late friend Commissioner Paul Elizondo had convinced me to run for a fifth term by stating that there are too many crazy people running for office. Brehm was clearly in need of assistance, so I said she was a good reason why Elizondo and I ran for re-election in 2018.

On May 25 a national poll was released that found 89 percent of Democrats supported a mask mandate but only 58 percent of Republicans supported it. President Trump, who had repeatedly refused to wear a mask and made fun of those who did, finally woke up after the poll and said that it was patriotic to wear one but that did not mean he would wear one.

In addition to masking up, Nirenberg and I had been encouraging people to get outside, savor nature, get some exercise, and enjoy a safe escape away from the virus. We had both led efforts to protect and restore our environment, create more green space, and build trails along the creeks and the San Antonio River.

I led the county effort to restore the eight-mile Mission Reach of the San Antonio River. It is known as the Mission Reach because of the four historic Spanish missions that lay alongside the river. The restoration was necessary because of the degradation of the eight-mile Mission Reach by the United States Army Corps of Engineers when they made it into a concrete drainage ditch.

The degradation of the river and its surrounding area over many years had resulted in the loss of biodiversity and the disruption of the ecosystem's structure. The destruction of surrounding trees and shrubs resulted in the capture of less carbon dioxide, a green-house gas emission that is causing our planet to heat up, leading to extreme weather conditions. Destruction of nature also increases the risk of pandemics. Greenhouse gases lead to poor air quality resulting in the spread of viruses.

In 2013 we completed the eight-mile river restoration, the largest environmental restoration of an urban river in the United States. When combined with adjacent city, county, and national parks, we have set aside 2,400 acres of nature, three times the size of Central Park in New York.

I mentioned in our May 21 media briefing that I had taken a hike along the Mission Reach of the river with former Mayor Phil Hardberger and Phil Bakke.

We walked along the hike-and-bike trails passing picnic sites and pavilions that Bexar County had funded. We passed some of the 13 acres of wetlands, 113 acres of aquatic habitat, and 334 acres of riparian habitat, as well as the 10,000 pounds of native grass and wildflower seeds and 20,000 trees that we planted. Each tree regulates the local climate, produces oxygen, improves soil quality, and absorbs 10 kilograms of carbon dioxide each year.

We sat for a while on a bench located in one of the pavilions overlooking the river watching herons dip down looking for fish and turtles basking in the sun. At the confluence of the river and San Pedro Creek is Confluence Park, opened in May 2018. It includes ecotype demonstration areas and a large-scale water catchment system.

It was a good day to get outside—a time to forget about COVID-19 and enjoy nature, a safe escape from the virus. We enjoyed our little animal friends who were flying, scampering, and swimming around.

The number of people taking hikes along the creek and river trails doubled during the pandemic, giving our citizens a safe environment to relieve the stress of the pandemic.

The *San Antonio Express-News* published an editorial on May 24 that I had written about the last four months of COVID-19. I emphasized that the COVID-19 crisis was not about "me" but "us" and that the vast majority of people recognized that we must respect each other to get through the pandemic.

I wrote that families were getting to know each other better as they worked at home and neighbors were taking walks or sitting on their front porches talking to each other. I stated that if we carried these principles forward, we could be a better society.

***

The five community action committees that Nirenberg and I appointed on March 30 presented their 38-page report that made recommendations regarding state and federal advocacy, philanthropy, food security and shelter, business and employment, and social services and health transition. The philanthropic committee, cochaired by Harvey Najim and Barbara Gentry, raised $15 million for housing and mental health issues.

The Federal and State Advocacy committee, co-chaired by

Councilman Manny Pelaez and Commissioner Kevin Wolff, obtained $40 million in grants for the airport and additional funds for other services.

The Food Security and Shelter committee, co-chaired by Commissioner Justin Rodriguez and Councilperson Jada Andrews-Sullivan, recommended $17.4 million for the food bank and the medically high-risk homeless population.

The Social Services Committee, co-chaired by Councilman Roberto Treviño and Commissioner Tommy Calvert, focused on the need for literacy efforts connected to job training.

The Business and Unemployment Committee, co-chaired by Councilperson Ana Sandoval and Commissioner Chico Rodriguez, recommended investments in skilled training. Their advice would be followed when both the city and county allocated funding from the CARES Act for job training.

The Economic Transition Committee, co-chaired by Kevin Voelkel and Julissa Carielo, provided a detailed plan for safety measures businesses should adopt during the COVID-19 pandemic.

The most important work was done by the Health Transition Team, chaired by Dr. Barbara Taylor, an infectious disease specialist with the UT Health System. Twelve other experts in infectious diseases, public health, community engagement, health equity, and medical ethics were members of the team. The team provided a comprehensive report that set safety and mitigation measures for schools, businesses, and other related activities. They also added measures to data accumulation to include, among other things, testing and hospitalization capacity. We would continue throughout the pandemic to consult with their leadership.

On May 31, 92 COVID-19 patients were in the hospital. It was a 66 percent increase since May 5 when the governor issued his emergency disarmament order. We were headed into the Memorial Day weekend, and that would be when we would find out if social gatherings would ignite a new surge.

Nirenberg and I had warned everybody that the gathering of family and friends over Memorial Day weekend could lead to an explosion of cases. Without the requirement to wear face coverings and no restrictions on the number of people who could gather, we knew we had a dangerous weekend ahead. The only step we could take was to restrict the number of people who could congregate in city and county parks and facilities—and we did so.

The Memorial Day weekend did not seem to bother Governor Abbott as he took another step in opening Texas, issuing a new emergency order effective June 3. It expanded restaurant capacity for all that were previously restricted to 25–50 percent. Later he announced another order allowing fine arts performance halls to operate indoors with 50 percent capacity. There were no limits on operating outdoors provided there was six feet of spacing between groups of 10 people. Two days later restaurants could expand to 75 percent capacity.

On our media briefing I quoted the famous philosopher, New York Yankee baseball catcher Yogi Berra, saying, "It ain't over till it's over." Nirenberg stated that Abbott wasn't heeding Berra's advice that, "If you don't know where you are going, you'll end up some place else."

We began to count the days after Memorial Day knowing that the spike could come after the 14-day incubation period was over. Sure enough, 14 days later we exceeded 100 COVID-19 patients in the hospital for the first time. Those 100 COVID-19 patients included 43 in ICU and 24 on ventilators.

Nirenberg and I kept warning people in our media briefings

that we were headed in the wrong direction. We kept pushing safety measures that people and businesses should take. But we were facing a difficult task as Democrats and Republicans were pulling apart.

The Pew Research Center conducted a survey from June 26–22 and found the divide between Democrats and Republicans was widening regarding the pandemic. Republicans said the worst was over (61 percent), and Democrats said the worst was still to come (82 percent). Only 45 percent of Republicans were concerned about spreading the virus as opposed to 77 percent of Democrats. Democrats were twice as likely as Republicans to say masks should be worn. Bipartisanship was quickly fading away.

***

While we were worried about gatherings that occurred over the Memorial Day weekend, we faced several large gatherings that began a few days later. On Saturday, May 29, a civil rights protest regarding the treatment of Black Americans by law enforcement officials began.

An estimated 5,000 demonstrators marched through the streets of downtown San Antonio to protest the alleged killing of George Floyd, a 46-year-old black man, who was arrested on May 25 in Minneapolis on suspicion of using a counterfeit $20 bill. Derek Chauvin, a white police officer with the Minneapolis Police Department, knelt on Floyd's neck for over nine minutes after he was handcuffed and lying face down. Floyd pleaded that he could not breathe but was ignored and he died.

There was a confrontation between some of the protesters and members of the Texas Freedom Force who were armed with assault-style rifles and shotguns guarding the white-marble Cenotaph in front of the Alamo, a monument to the Alamo defenders. Police formed a barrier between members of the Freedom Force and the civil rights marchers. One row of officers used their bikes to separate the groups; a second row stood with batons in their hands. Police escorted militia members away from the area.

As Alamo Plaza began to clear out, people began rioting on East Houston Street. As a crowd of people broke a storefront window at a jewelry store, police officers released tear gas and sprayed small pellet-like objects into the crowd.

By 10:30 p.m., the contested section of Houston Street appeared to be cleared of thugs but was left littered with garbage. Shards of glass scattered across the pavement glittered under the streetlights.

Because of the violence, Nirenberg issued a disaster declaration for the city and issued a temporary curfew effective 11:30 p.m. on Saturday until 6:00 a.m. on Monday, June 1, 2020.

On Tuesday, I stood with civil rights protesters who had gathered on the courthouse plaza around Lady Justice standing in the middle of the courtyard on a globe above the restored 1896 12-foot-high cast iron fountain. In one hand, she has the scales of justice and in the other a sword, representing the enforcement of justice. She is blindfolded representing objectivity. She has a ribbon in a curvilinear form floating above her head to represent the sky.

My wife Tracy had raised money to sculpt Lady Justice through the Hidalgo Foundation she had created. The sculpture was based on Praxiteles' "Aphrodite of Knidos," the Goddess of Love. Aphrodite taught a message of love as the most important component of justice. Symbols are important and none is more important than what Lady Justice represents.

I watched and listened to speakers who were standing on the ascending spacious granite steps of the courthouse. The speakers were flanked by immense granite columns and bronze lamps. Two corner towers, one topped by a beehive dome and the other a rectangular shape with a hipped roof, were on each side of the stairs.

The protest was handled properly by Bexar County Sheriff Javier Salazar who empathized with the protesters. "Black lives do matter," Salazar said in front of the group. During the exchange, Salazar told demonstrators about anti-racism protocols he had put in effect to ensure fairness in his office and spoke about efforts to ensure his deputies were ethnically diverse. Salazar and several deputies then joined the march.

The next day while the protest was mostly peaceful, a small group came to a face-off with police officers around 11:00 p.m. near Alamo Plaza. The demonstration escalated and officers used pepper balls, smoke, and wooden and rubber projectiles as protesters ran away. In response to the incident, Nirenberg announced that he had initiated a review of the city's role in the criminal justice system, including the use of force, to ensure the equitable treatment of communities of color.

The following day on June 3, the marchers arrived downtown around 4:00 p.m. Among those participating were San Antonio Spurs players Lonnie Walker and Bryn Forbes and former Spur Sean Elliott. By the time nighttime fell, most of the protesters had left, except for a group that remained at Travis Park until at least 11:00 p.m. Mayor Ron Nirenberg issued another temporary curfew for the downtown business district and Alamo Plaza that would last until June 7.

The next day on June 4, the sixth day of protests, Mayor Nirenberg delivered a passionate speech to the protesters in the courthouse plaza. He said, "We hear you. We know there needs to be change. I will be working every single day until everybody goes home and feels like they don't have to fight for something that God gave them to begin with, which is freedom to feel safe in their own community....I'm asking you to hold me accountable...nobody else. Because I am the mayor of this...city and we're going to make change together."

For the next few days, the marches were peaceful and drew less people each day until they eventually came to an end. Overall the marches and protests were mostly peaceful except for the few that vandalized Houston Street.

I believe San Antonio's police and Bexar County Sheriff's deputies used restraint and did an overall great job of preventing any dangerous escalation of violence. They were on the frontline throughout the pandemic. Across the nation, more than 460 American law enforcement officers have died from COVID-19 tied to their work since the pandemic began. More than four times as many officers died from COVID-19 as from gun fire.

Over the next several weeks, the city announced a series of police reforms, including the elimination of no-knock warrants and chokeholds, along with a sweeping collective bargaining agenda that sought to improve accountability and transparency in the discipline process for police accused of misconduct.

Nirenberg and I were criticized for not banning the demonstrations because of an uptick in COVID-19 cases. We understood gatherings could lead to super spreaders of COVID-19, but we supported their right to peacefully protest as long as they observed health safety measures and were outside in a safe environment against COVID-19. When things got out of hand, police did take charge and broke up the unruly protesters.

While the days of the civil rights protest were diverting public attention away from COVID-19, signs were increasing that we were headed for trouble. We had blunted the first COVID-19 attack and received very little damage, but our victory would prove to be illusive. Disarmament that began with the governor's May 5 emergency order had provided Mr. COVID the opening he was looking for.

4. Summertime Tsunami

On June 11 Metro Health Director Dawn Emerick joined us on our daily media briefing. She stated that we were entering an increasing wave of COVID-19 cases and attributed the rise in cases to social gatherings over the Memorial Day weekend and the stripping of safeguards by the governor. "Take this seriously," she warned.

Nirenberg and I stated that we should not count on vaccines to save us because the Phase 3 vaccine trails underway would take six to eight months to complete. We predicted they would become available during the first quarter of 2021.

So, we emphasized the need to mask up, keep social distances, and beware of the unseen Mr. COVID who was everywhere. Small businesses needed to be prepared for what we thought would be another wave of COVID-19.

To assist small businesses, I helped by handing out plexiglass shields to owners of small businesses as they passed by in their cars and pickups in the parking lot of the Bexar County Expo Hall. We followed up later by distributing one million masks to small businesses.

On June 12 I wrote a letter to Governor Abbott asking him

to allow local officials to impose a mandatory face covering order. I stated that because his emergency order did away with face covering mandates, fewer people were wearing them and the rate of infections were increasing.

The letter became public, and the governor responded through the media stating that I believed in government mandates and he in individual responsibility. Of course, individual freedom is not threatened by mandatory safety measures. We are required to wear seat belts, cannot text while driving, must conform to speed limits, give turn signals, and turn on our lights at night while driving. Wearing a face covering during a deadly pandemic is hardly a great imposition on individual freedom. At this point the governor was riding high and saw no need to put in mandatory health measures.

In June, Bexar Facts, a non-profit organization organized by political consultant Christian Archer who had managed my campaigns, ran a poll that included job approval ratings.

The polling showed strong bipartisan support and Abbott and me at the same percentage (61 percent). Nirenberg, who runs in a non-partisan election, rated 67 percent. But the ratings would change as summertime would reveal the huge blunder Abbott made in doing away with public health safeguards.

As things continued to get worse across the state, health officials increased pressure on the governor to take action. He was caught in a box between health experts' advice and the right wing of his political party.

On June 16 Governor Abbott was quoted in the newspaper as saying that counties and cities had not done enough to require businesses to comply with health protocols. Was this a riddle waiting for someone to solve it? If so, what was the answer?

The attorney general's letter of May 12 stated that our previous emergency order that required businesses to provide face masks was invalid and unenforceable. Did the governor intend to overrule the attorney general?

On that same day I talked with Craig Boyan, CEO of H-E-B grocery stores. He said businesses were caught in a no-win position by having to decide whether to require a face covering or not. Either way they chose, many customers got mad at them. They preferred a government mandate that they were required to follow. Boyan stated that he had conveyed that wish to the governor's office.

Putting all the pieces together, I recognized that the governor would more than likely respond to business leaders rather than health officials. So, was the reason for the riddle to let local officials figure it out and take the political heat?

Later that day I met with County Manager David Smith and Assistant District Attorney Larry Roberson, who drafted my emergency orders. Smith said, "The governor did use the word 'require' in reference to business safety measures."

Roberson commented that he didn't know how far I could go in requiring a business to enact safety measures. I responded that I wanted to go as far as possible. After a thorough discussion, I decided to draw up an emergency order that required all commercial entities providing direct goods and services to the public to develop and implement a health and safety policy that included, at a minimum, that all employees or visitors must wear face coverings. The policy notice had to be posted in a conspicuous location to provide notice to employees and visitors. A fine, not to exceed $1,000 per violation, would be assessed to those businesses that failed to comply. I decided I wanted to issue it tomorrow.

I waited until the following morning to call Mayor Nirenberg and invite him to a quick media conference that I called to be held in the Commissioners Court chambers. He accepted.

We met in a small conference room next to the Commissioners Court chambers. I explained the order and apologized for the late notice. I told him I kept it secret because the order clearly conflicts with the attorney general's opinion and goes beyond the governor's order.

I said, "I did not believe the city attorney would authorize this action for the city to take because the order might well be thrown out by the courts." Nirenberg replied that he was glad I was taking this action.

At the press conference, Nirenberg and I were joined by District Attorney Joe Gonzales. I explained the emergency order and then said, "I might be pushing the legal bounds a bit, but I believe we can defend this order in court." The order would take effect the following Monday. Mayor Nirenberg spoke in favor of the order and stated, "We have got to get used to doing the right thing when we are out in the public."

At noon I had lunch at J. Alexanders with my political consultant Christian Archer, prominent trial attorney Mikal Watts, Assistant Attorney General Paul Singer, and Assistant District Attorney Larry Roberson. We had gathered to talk about a proposed settlement in the case we had filed against the pharmacy companies that had manufactured opioids and marketed them to people who ended up addicted, many of them dying from overdoses.

As we were talking about the case, Archer looked up from his phone and said, "The governor just told a Waco news station that Wolff finally figured it out. He said he will not challenge your emergency order. I guess you are good at solving riddles."

Texas Monthly magazine would later give Governor Abbott one of their annual Bum Steer awards for his obfuscation riddle and gave me credit for breaking the code. On the social media comments, someone said that the governor was acting the part of the Riddler from the Batman shows.

Solving the riddle was cause for a celebration and I was elated as the news quickly spread throughout the state. Eventually the county judges and mayors of the six largest counties and cities began to issue similar orders. After getting clearance from the governor, Mayor Nirenberg announced during the media briefing that night that he was issuing a similar order.

It would take some time before the measure had any effect. Businesses would have to develop a health policy, post it, and require their customers to wear a mask. Meanwhile we were in for a very rough time.

At our media briefing that day Nirenberg and I stated that things were getting much worse. In the last 17 days the number of hospitalizations had increased by 600 percent (from 84 to 518 patients). ICU patients were up 400 percent and those on ventilators by 500 percent.

When a patient reaches the point of having to enter intensive care and be put on a ventilator it is a danger sign that they may not survive. Thanks to a large-scale clinical trial in Great Britain released on June 16, they found that dexamethasone, a generic corticosteroid drug, reduced deaths by one-fifth among COVID-19 patients needing supplemental oxygen. Early on, the CDC did not recommend using it because it could suppress the immune system, but the new study found it was helpful when given later as the disease progressed in severity.

At our media briefings we stated that health officials had warned that our local hospitals could be filled up in two weeks. We warned that people had become too lax and complacent about taking proactive measures, and we pleaded with them to wear face coverings and keep six feet apart. I asked them to remember "Ubuntu," explaining that it was a Zulu term meaning "humanity for others."

The following day all the hospitals stated they were implementing a new policy that visitors would not be allowed in the hospital to see a COVID-19 patient because of the fear of passing the virus to visitors. It was a necessary restriction, but it would have a negative impact on loved ones who wanted to be with their friends or family members. The new policy resulted in many COVID-19 patients dying alone.

***

On June 24 when I entered Lowes Home Improvement Center, I noticed my new order on the door requiring face coverings. When I looked at my name on the order, I thought I would be in for a lot of criticism. But it would be much worse.

As I was standing in line, I saw a customer arguing with the cashier when he told him he would not check him out because he did not have a face covering. He was a big guy, about six foot two inches, in his forties with a t-shirt bearing an American flag, an assault weapon, and "Combat Iron" stenciled on the front.

I went up to him, started to hand him my card, and told him that the store was complying with a local order that required face coverings. He hit me on my wrist, knocked the card out of my hand, and angrily stated that he would not obey a local order. He proceeded to cuss me out.

Since he was about half my age and twice as big, I decided that as a 79-year-old guy I should call the sheriff. I put Sheriff Salazar on my speaker phone and let him hear what the guy was saying. Later the Sheriff said, "I could hear the subject berating the judge."

As he walked out of the store, I followed him to his pickup and wrote down his license plate number. The sheriff and several deputies arrived after he left and took statements.

He was arrested the next day and booked. By now I had cooled down and realized that I should not press charges because all I was going to do was make a hero out of him to his far-right followers. I stated to the media that I believed he had just had a bad day and that I had been trying to solve the conflict, but it had not worked out so well.

Because I did not want to file charges, District Attorney (DA) Joe Gonzales charged him with disorderly conduct (a misdemeanor). But this charge would also give notoriety so eventually the DA dropped the charges.

Later Lowes released a video tape of the encounter, and I was relieved to see it because it confirmed my statement of what happened. The *Daily Beast* ran a story about the incident. It stated that my "signature bandana might make you think of the Wild West and the likes of Roy Bean, the long ago 'hanging judge' of Val Verde County in Texas." The article stated that "Wolff is a figure such as is desperately needed during this pandemic."

***

Abbott finally realized he had to do something as COVID-19 was spreading around the state. On June 25 he said the numbers had completely spiked and that the reopening of the Texas economy could be in jeopardy. The following day he closed bars, prohibited rafting and tubing, and limited outdoor gatherings to 100, but with numerous exceptions including churches.

It was a good step for the governor to take, but the order was too weak and too late to stem the tide. By now COVID-19 was flashing everywhere, causing havoc and fear. It would take us time to develop a shield that could block the penetrating flash of COVID-19, but vaccines were still a long way off. So, we continued to plead with people to take safety measures as we geared up to enforce our new emergency order requiring businesses to require face masks at a minimum.

On June 25 we held a virtual conference with officials from Navistar to announce the groundbreaking of a 900,000 sq. ft. manufacturing facility for medium and heavy-duty trucks. Chairman Troy Clarke said there was a lot of uncertainty but not about their commitment to build the plant in San Antonio.

Navistar was a major victory for San Antonio during a time of so much uncertainty as to what would happen to our economy after COVID-19. Later they would announce the moving of their engineering division to San Antonio to be located on a nearby location to their manufacturing plant.

Well, that was one good day, but the next day was not so good. City Manager Erik Walsh informed us that Metro Health Director Dawn Emerick had resigned. Emerick had been on the job since January 27, 2020, arriving at the beginning of the outbreak of COVID-19. Thrust into a very difficult job, Emerick reached a breaking point after serving some five months. She said, "I'm angry, I'm tired, and it shouldn't be this way." She added that the pandemic was wreaking havoc on the staff throughout the entire system.

No local public health organization could have foreseen the pandemic coming in the form that it did. These organizations had to deal with misinformation from the start when the CDC announced that they thought there was little chance COVID-19 would result in a major spread. Originally, the CDC confused them when they said face coverings were not necessary. They also had to deal with political figures, like President Trump, who failed to take their advice.

Fortunately, Assistant City Manager Dr. Colleen Bridger, who had previously headed up Metro Health, stepped in to take charge. She quickly settled everyone down and hired additional people.

When hospital systems across the state began reaching a stress point, Governor Abbott limited elective surgeries to free up more beds for COVID-19 patients. At the same time Nirenberg and I began pushing the state to start staffing up the 250-bed field hospital at the Freeman Coliseum for COVID-19 patients.

We received push back from the leaders of our hospital systems who said it was best to treat COVID-19 patients within the four walls of the hospitals where they had all the services necessary to treat them. They suggested that the field hospital be used for other patients that had less of a need for comprehensive services. They were right.

To keep patients within the four walls of the hospital required more staff. The Federal Emergency Management Agency (FEMA) agreed to reimburse the cost for additional staff.

***

On June 29 early voting began for the run-off elections. Governor Abbott made a wise move when he extended early voting from five days to ten. This helped prevent overcrowding of the polling locations, but there was still concern that people would show up without face coverings, so we encouraged voters who were eligible to vote by mail to do so. I made it clear to voters that the Texas Supreme Court ruled that it was up to them individually to decide if they had a health condition that made it dangerous for them to vote in person.

Bexar County Election Administer Jacque Callanen invited

me to address the election judges to explain the steps we were taking to protect them from COVID-19. I told them while the governor prohibited us from mandating face masks for voters, we would provide them with masks, gloves, and plastic shields and would sanitize all the equipment. I said I would understand if they chose not to man the polls. Even though their average age was 72 most of them decided to work.

Two days after early voting began, we had 1,268 new COVID-19 cases reported and 966 COVID-19 patients in local hospitals. I stated on our show that we were in an extraordinarily dangerous time. Nirenberg stated that our hospital capacity could run out in the next week or two, even with the assignment of 565 traveling nurses to our local hospitals.

Almost every day I communicated with UHS President George Hernandez as hospitalization continued to climb. Even though the Commissioners Court had approved $900 million in financing and taxes to build our new state-of-the-art 10-story hospital, there still was not enough capacity.

Looking ahead to population growth and future pandemics, we would need more hospital capacity. Hernandez said that we needed to build a couple of new community hospitals in the growing areas of Bexar County. He began to look for sites.

A few months later, UHS purchased 80 acres located in west Bexar County for $13.4 million and 42.5 acres located in northeast Bexar County for $11.5 million. These two investments would provide us the sites for future hospitals.

***

The July 4 weekend was upon us, and we expected another outbreak like the one we experienced on Memorial Day weekend.

We warned everyone that conditions would get worse after the holiday if they gathered in groups. We pointed to new findings by Georgia Tech researchers who found that on average if 25 people gathered, there was a 68 percent chance of someone having COVID-19 and 90 percent chance if 100 or more.

To control gatherings, we imposed a limit of 10 people at a gathering and warned people that police and deputies would break up any groups exceeding 10. We also closed all our parks and warned people to keep a social distance of six feet and wear a face covering.

In early July, Assistant City Manager Dr. Colleen Bridger began to ramp up contact tracing. She arranged for space in the Alamodome and began hiring more people to expand from 70 to 175 contact tracers. The contact tracers asked those infected for the location where they likely picked up the virus. They also asked them to call people they had been in contact with and ask them to self-quarantine for 14 days. It was a difficult job locating people and then convincing them to share information.

On July 2, Dr. Ian Thompson, CEO of Santa Rosa Hospital, appeared on our show and said the pandemic was breathtaking given the 1,074 patients in hospital, including 332 in intensive care and 180 on ventilators. He pleaded with people to follow our advice.

For the first time we issued an emergency alert to all cell phones on July 3. Over the period of the pandemic, we would use emergency alerts selectively. We warned everybody that infections were increasing and that Governor Abbott had just mandated face covering and imposed a $250 fine for violators. But again, it was another weak order because he required a warning on the first offense. The order was almost impossible to enforce because of the improbability of the same officer running into the same offender twice. The anti-face-mask crowd understood they would never be fined. But at least his order sent a message that people should wear a face covering.

In our July 7 media briefing, I presented Mayor Nirenberg with a framed painting of the two of us. He was wearing a mask and me a bandanna. The painting was a nice keepsake for Nirenberg and me, and it's on the cover of this book.

I thanked Sara Barcus, the artist, who was a student of teacher Kristopher Wickerham, who had purchased the original. Wickerham is married to Kathy Bieser, principal of CAST Tech High School, who I had met in 2020 when we began building a new BiblioTech library on the downtown San Antonio Independent School District's Fox Tech campus. The campus also includes the Health and Law High School and the Advance Learning Academy.

The new BiblioTech EDU building on the Fox Tech campus.

Tracy and I dine frequently at our favorite neighborhood café, Pam's. Locally owned by Pam and David Strain, they kept the

Barcus painting displayed throughout the pandemic.

While Nirenberg and I relied on the advice of health experts, there were times when we had to push back. We had a little dust up when they recommended that we require all businesses to do temperature checks before people entered. We thought it would cause more problems than it solved by causing people to bunch up in lines to enter large stores like H-E-B, Target, and Walmart. Instead of mandating temperature checks for all businesses, Nirenberg and I encouraged business with limited traffic to do so.

As our COVID-19 hospital patients continued to rise, Nirenberg and I appealed to Brooke Army Medical Center to allow COVID-19 patients to be treated in their hospital. They had a history of treating civilians who had been injured in car crashes or wounded in a violent confrontation. While local military officers wanted to help, the big dogs in the Trump administration would not let them.

On the positive side, the military had established strong health safety measures for military and civilian personnel who worked on base. That was good because many of them lived outside the base and interacted with all our citizens.

Army North, commanded by Lt. General Laura J. Richardson, is a nationwide command headquartered at Joint Base San Antonio. Army North sent thousands of medical teams to six states to fill critical gaps in COVID-19 care.

By mid-July we had exceeded 200 COVID-19 deaths and the count was growing daily and putting a strain on funeral homes. Some hospitals had to start preparing to hold bodies in refrigerated trucks until the morgue or funeral home could pick them up.

On the day before the July 14 run-off election, we hit a high of 1,267 COVID-19 patients in the hospital. It was a dangerous time for people to be standing in line because Abbott's order prevented us from mandating face masks at polling sites. We took all the safety precautions we could, and fortunately, the run-off election drew a small crowd of voters.

In the Republican runoff, much to my delight, Trish De-Berry defeated Tom Rickhoff 54.33 percent to 45.67 percent. As expected in the Democratic primary, Rebeca Clay-Flores defeated Commissioner Chico Rodriguez 61.77 percent to 38.23 percent. They would both have to run in the November general election, but DeBerry was in a safe Republican district and Clay-Flores in a very strong Democratic district.

We knew as we headed toward the November 2020 general elections that several hundred thousand voters would cast their ballots. If COVID-19 was still prevalent we could run into serious problems.

***

On July 14 my friend and the county emergency management coordinator Kyle Coleman died of COVID-19. He was a great public servant who had led the county through countless natural disasters throughout his years of service. He had led the COVID-19 effort to set up testing sites, distribute PPE, and respond to emergency calls for help.

During our evening television show I read his wife's statement that she hoped his death would bring attention to the need to wear masks and practice social distancing. I later spoke at his funeral on the grounds of the Freeman Coliseum to hundreds of people sitting in their cars who had come to pay their respects.

***

Bexar County Medical Examiner Dr. Kimberly Molina reported another seven COVID-19 deaths on July 16, bringing the total to 22 that she had certified after an autopsy. It takes time to perform an autopsy so there was a lag in reporting these deaths. When a death occurs in a hospital, the attending doctor certifies the cause of death, and the information is almost immediately available.

On the same day Dr. Paul Hancock, chief medical officer for Methodist Health Care, appeared on our daily show. He said he was nervous to see their emergency rooms very quiet. People who needed urgent care were not seeking help because of a fear of COVID-19. He assured everyone that it was safe and there was no reason to be concerned about being exposed to COVID-19.

The emergency order that we enacted regarding mandates on businesses to post safety protocols, including a face covering mandate, was finally beginning to have an impact. On our July 18 media briefing, Nirenberg stated that in the last five days COVID-19 hospital patients declined by 123. I said that I thought we were on a slow road to recovery and our hospital patient numbers would continue to go down.

While older people were most susceptible to having COVID-19, our numbers had now begun to show cases among younger people rising. Children under 18 accounted for one in ten COVID-19 cases, of which 200 were infants. It was clear that no one was safe from COVID-19.

With rising cases among children, on July 17 Metro Health Medical Director Dr. Junda Woo ordered public schools to keep students out of classrooms and prohibit in-person school-sponsored events, including athletics. Under her proposed order classroom attendance would be delayed until September and would depend on an assessment at that time regarding whether to continue.

The order led to a lot of confusion. Two outlying school districts headquartered in Kendall County and Comal County had schools within Bexar County. Their school officials said they were not going along with the order.

Private religious schools also rebelled. Cornerstone Church pastors John Hagee and his son Matthew sued to keep their schools open. Attorney General Paxton issued an advisory opinion that the health authority had no power to close schools.

Nirenberg and I asked the governor to resolve the issue. Two weeks later he responded that local public health officials have no authority to close schools. Regardless, Nirenberg and I encouraged schools to hold off having in-person classes until September.

On our July 23 show, I went public with the failure of the state to pick up jail inmates who were paper ready to be transferred to prison. We had over 300 jail inmates who should have been transferred to prison. The state had a COVID-19 problem in the prison system, so they decided the best way to solve it was to jam up our jails, causing us to face a serious COVID-19 problem. As our jail population grew because of their refusal to accept prisoners, we were running out of room to separate new inmates for the 14-day incubation period as well as those affected by COVID-19.

A few days later, Governor Abbott compounded our jail problems by issuing a new emergency order that prevented us from giving a personal recognizance bond to those charged with misdemeanors because somewhere in the deep past they had a violent incident. It did not matter how long ago or how serious the incident was. Eventually our jail population would grow from just under 3,000 to almost 4,000. The governor was creating a dangerous environment for COVID-19 to spread. I wrote letters protesting the failure of the state to pick up paper-ready inmates. I should have saved the paper and the postage. No answer.

The governor's action, and later his pushing of legislation favored by the bail bond industry, would also destroy so much; we had worked to heal and treat people rather than incarcerate them. Jails are a medieval institution trying to solve modern society problems by criminalizing people who have mental and drug addiction problems. Since I became county judge in 2001, we have successfully instituted therapeutic justice rather than incarcerating sick people who are non-violent offenders.

We first created the Office of Criminal Justice, presided over by Mike Lozito, to implement therapeutic justice. Over the years we have created 14 therapeutic courts that include mental health courts, additional drug courts, a veteran's court, a DWI court, a PEARLS court helping women caught up in human trafficking, and an EAGLES court helping young boys in foster care.

Some of those convicted of a crime who were serving time and had exhibited good behavior were transferred to long-term drug and mental health treatments at our Applewhite Recovery Center. I have been to the center on various occasions to meet and talk with inmates. I had our BiblioTech library provide them with e-book readers and access to thousands of e-books.

We also established a mental health diversion program, giving the police an opportunity to take an arrested person to a mental health facility rather than jail. We created a restoration program to help build a pathway for inmates who have served their time. We opened a comprehensive center near the jail that provides housing, job search resources, treatment, and other services. We have also established a public defender office with 22 attorneys for indigent defendants.

We instituted a magistration process at the jail that would

require the public defender and the DA to be at all magistrate hearings. They would give priority to personal recognizance bonds for low-level offenses rather than resorting to the bail bond industry. Before the person is brought before the magistrate, they have a mental health assessment.

In 2003, my wife Tracy raised money to build a 10,000 sq. ft. state-of-the-art children's court on the third floor of the courthouse that included an early intervention court and a family drug court to help families stabilize rather than taking the children away and possibly incarcerating the parents. Families were provided wraparound services to help families become stable and keep their children.

Over the last 20 years of instituting therapeutic justice, we have saved numerous lives and reduced our jail population, thus saving taxpayers millions of dollars. I believe all our actions also had a positive impact during the COVID-19 epidemic by rehabilitating people and saving them from the mental trauma of COVID-19. Now the governor was putting all efforts to heal in jeopardy.

***

As I stated earlier it was almost impossible to enforce Abbott's mask order because of the necessity of a warning and then finding the same person again. By now, 3,790 calls had been made to police complaining about people who were not wearing masks.

It was a different story with businesses. Inspections found that almost all were abiding by our local order because it was in their best interest to protect their employees and customers. Those few that were not complying were given a warning and later were followed up with inspections by deputies and police. Again, we found compliance in most cases and accessed fines if they did not comply. Over time, it would prove that one of the safest places you could be was in a business establishment that followed our emergency orders.

By July 25 we felt comfortable enough to state on our media briefing that we were hopeful and encouraged by the drop of patients in the hospital (220 less patients than our highest count). We were also feeling good about our percent positivity going from a high of 22 percent of those tested the previous week down to 17.7 percent. Mayor Nirenberg stated that the trend was in the right direction, but it was going to be a slow decline. With 1,050 people in the hospital, we both stated that it was not time to let our guard down.

As the month of August progressed, our hospital numbers continued to slowly come down. At our media briefing I talked about my visit to La Cantera Mall where people stopped me and thanked Mayor Nirenberg and me for the job we were doing. Almost everyone I passed had a face covering on.

But while our hospital numbers continued to come down, the number of deaths increased because many of our citizens had underlying health conditions such as diabetes, obesity, and heart disease. Many of our patients who had fought the silent reaper began to lose their battle.

On our August 3 briefing I emphasized that no single health safety intervention was enough. People needed to layer up, including keeping a physical distance, wearing a face covering, cleaning hands, and sanitizing surfaces.

Nirenberg stated that continued testing and tracking was necessary to find where infections occurred as well as then isolating people who had who tested positive and quarantining those who had been exposed.

On August 4 Nirenberg and I met Governor Abbott at the private airport Million Air located on the northern edge of the San Antonio Airport. At the time we still had 838 COVID-19 patients in the hospital.

We were escorted into a room where we were required to take a COVID-19 test before we joined the governor in an adjoining room. I thought this was strange as I had never been required to take a test before meeting with someone.

Nirenberg pressed him on the need for mandatory health safety measures. I told him about the effect of his emergency order on restricting personal recognize bonds and how it resulted in a dangerous situation in jails as we were overloaded with non-violent misdemeanor offenders.

Governor Abbott is a charming guy who speaks to you rather than talks with you. So, there was no give and take on the issues we presented. He listened but did not commit to supporting any of our requests. Instead, he expressed his confidence that we were on the downside of the surge, life would get back to normal, and no further action was necessary.

On our August 11 briefing, we explained why labs were taking so long to deliver results. The labs were facing a demand to deliver millions of test results while they had limited chemicals, machines, and kits for the tests. One of the labs, Quest, suggested that we reduce testing people without symptoms. But that was bad advice as asymptomatic people were spreading the virus nearly as much as those who had symptoms.

Questions were asked about why some people do not get sick from the virus. It was estimated that 40 percent of those infected had no symptoms or mild ones. We stated that they may have received a low viral load, they were young and had an immunity or partial immunity, or they just were blessed with great genes.

The good news was those that did have COVID-19, whether they had symptoms or not, could develop antibodies to help prevent further short-term infections. Later we would learn that infection did not offer the same level of protection as vaccines. Eventually with vaccinations we hoped to stop the spread of COVID-19.

Texas Biomedical Research Institute CEO Larry Schlesinger came on our daily briefing show on August 21. He stated there were 165 COVID-19 vaccines in development, of which 32 were in clinical trials and eight in large Phase 3 trials. He was encouraged by the massive effort, but we were still months away from getting a vaccine approved.

On the following day I reminded everyone that it had taken us two months to bring COVID-19 hospitalizations down to 530 patients, while it took only about three weeks during the summer spike for COVID-19 to reach 1,267 hospitalizations. We warned everyone to beware of a possible unrestrained, furious return of COVID-19.

***

As I mentioned earlier, the COVID-19 epidemic led to many people living alone who were susceptible to mental challenges. Too often calls for help were responded to by law enforcement rather than mental health experts.

On August 25 three deputies responded to a call from the Red Cross requesting assistance for Damian Lamar Daniels, a veteran. They knew he had mental problems because deputies had been to his house the day before. This time they got into a physical confrontation, and Daniels was shot two times in the chest and killed. Daniels had a gun under his shirt.

After a review of the information on August 28, I stated that this incident should have never happened. Daniels had a right to have a gun at his residence—he did not have a criminal record, there was no warrant for his arrest, and no mental health order was issued to seize him.

County Manager David Smith, at my request, assigned our Mental Health Department the task of conducting a review of the handling of this case and of making recommendations for policy changes.

After receiving the report, I then persuaded the Commissioners Court to approve $1.5 million in funding to create a mobile mental health unit consisting of a mental health clinician, an emergency medical technician, and a trained plain-clothes deputy.

The unit was put under the direction of South Texas Regional Advisory Council, an organization that coordinates transportation to hospitals and various other health care institutions. Two days later the San Antonio Police Department announced a new policy that they would respond to a mental health crisis with a mental health team.

Over the next year the mobile unit responded to 378 mental health calls and followed up with 143 visits. All the responses were successful and without any violence. As a result of our success, we expanded our services by adding personnel and extending the unit to two response teams. This was a major step in handling so many mental health calls, caused in part by COVID-19 stress.

***

On August 26, we reported that our positivity rate dipped below 10 percent and we were down to 436 in the hospital from a high of 1,267 on July 14. This brought us down to a moderate level from the red zone of July. Even though we were going in the right direction we took the precaution of closing parks over the upcoming Labor Day weekend.

Mayor Nirenberg revealed a model from the health care

intelligence company Sg2 that predicted a continuing decline in COVID-19 cases through September. They had predicted the summer spike, so they had credibility.

On that same day, while the COVID-19 news was good, we had an emergency to deal with. Our Bexar County Exposition Hall and surrounding grounds is the emergency center for any natural disaster that happens in South Texas. Evacuees began arriving from South Texas due to a possible hurricane coming their way. They would be arriving at the same time we were testing for COVID-19 at the Expo Hall, so we set up a large tent facility to check them in.

I drove out to the center passing hundreds of cars that were lined up to check in. Most were sent to some 535 hotel rooms that were reserved for them around the city. However, some were sick and our empty field hospital in the Expo Hall began to fill up. Walking through the field hospital, I stopped to talk to some of the 78 patients. They were appreciative of our services.

But guess what. The hurricane never arrived. People who were sent to hotels were able to stay a week for a free vacation in the Alamo city.

***

As we headed into the Labor Day weekend, Nirenberg and I sounded the alarms reminding people how the virus spread during the Memorial Day and July 4th weekends. We asked people to avoid gathering with others outside their households, to keep social distance, and wear a face covering.

We were pleased that The University of Texas at San Antonio President Taylor Eighmy told us he was taking no chances of letting his student body become a super spreader. He knew young people were twice as likely as older adults to infect others because of their social interactions. For the upcoming fall semester, 95 percent of his students would take online courses with only 2,000 staff and students returning to the campus. Normally the university would have 32,000 students and 4,500 staff on their two campuses. Texas A&M–San Antonio President Cynthia Teniente-Matson announced that only 10 percent of courses would be in person.

Metro Health Medical Director Dr. Woo, who had lost in her attempt to close K–12 schools and keep kids in virtual learning, presented the schools with a list of safeguards they should implement. She also established a stress level for schools that ranged from high risk to low and was color coded red, yellow, and green. Within a month of school openings, she declared them a "low risk" zone.

NISD Superintendent Brian Woods struggled with planning for the beginning of the 2020 school year. He became frustrated with the TEA over their indecision of how to fund the cost of online students. He had already purchased tens of millions of dollars' worth of technology for students and staff and an online learning management system, but the rules were not issued until a couple of weeks before school started when the TEA issued rules regarding online learning as well as funding.

NISD began the school year completely virtual. In the second week they brought back students in Pre-K and Kindergarten as well as some with special needs and English language learners. Woods slowly ramped up in-person attendance throughout the fall of 2020.

***

I had lunch with Rackspace founder Graham Weston, Kronkosky Foundation President Tullos Wells, and Tobin Foundation Chairman Bruce Bugg on September 4. We dined at Club Giraud to talk about a new venture the three of them were planning. First Graham told us about how he contracted COVID-19 when he was infected by his asymptomatic 22-year-old son. He told me, "I had fever, chills, and chest pain. I had a hard time breathing and a pain in my lungs. I thought I was going to die. I recovered but it took me a week to start feeling better."

His personal experience led him to join with Bugg and Wells to launch Community Labs, a COVID-PCR testing process that included a nostril swab to get a sample, with the results of the test given within 24 hours. His idea was to test asymptomatic people in a cohort setting who might be carrying the virus and unknowingly passing it on to others. He wanted to test school children and faculty every week to provide a safe environment for children to return to school. The cost would be $35 per test.

I told them I thought it was a good idea but that it was going to be very expensive with thousands of children in school in Bexar County. He suggested a pilot program in one of our small school districts and said he would need help in funding the initiative. I asked that they arrange a tour for commissioners at their lab located in the South Texas Blood and Tissue Center.

Two weeks later they went public with their plan after they reached an agreement with the superintendent of Somerset High School, Saul Hinojosa, to begin the program; in this school the student body was 95 percent Hispanic.

When I talked with Hinojosa, he was excited about the program. Only about 30 percent of his 4,000 students were returning to school because of fear of COVID-19. It was feared more in the Hispanic community because of the high number of deaths Hispanics experienced due to high rates of obesity, diabetes, and heart disease. Hinojosa thought the testing program would encourage parents to let their kids return to school.

Later, the Commissioners Court approved two million dollars in grants to Community Labs to pay for half the cost of each test. We were the first to step up to help finance Community Labs. As Graham moved on to include other school districts, we provided additional funding, bringing our total up to $4 million.

***

On our September 5 media briefing, I talked about the safety measures we had implemented in the county building. Under the leadership of Director of Facilities Dan Curry, we installed UV lamps on both sides of where the air enters and exits the air vents. We deployed HEPA scrubbing machines in our congregate settings and high traffic locations. We adjusted our HVAC controls to increase the air changes per hour in our building to an average of four to six. I urged other businesses to do the same and emphasized to homeowners to keep fresh air circulating in their homes.

By the middle of September our positivity rate was down to 6 percent. There were 228 COVID-19 patients in the hospitals, down from a high of 1,267 patients on July 13. With the slowdown of COVID-19 transmissions less people were getting tested. Mayor Nirenberg announced that our testing capacity remained five times over our current need.

As fall approached, it seemed after blunting COVID-19 in the spring and then finally curtailing the devastating summer tsunami, we may not have another surge. We worked our way through the summer surge with limited local control imposed by the governor's emergency orders. But we paid a high price in lost lives and long-term negative effects for many people struck with COVID-19. By the middle of September, there were 1,019 of our citizens that had died due to COVID-19.

While Nirenberg and I continued to urge citizens to practice health safety protocols, we began to return to a somewhat normal life. People were looking forward to taking their kids trick-or-treating and, a month later, eating turkey with the family on Thanksgiving Day. All was good it seemed.

5. Fall-Time Complacency

WITH COVID-19 SEEMINGLY under control it was time to focus on reviving our economy and pushing forward with capital projects to build our city. The city and county budgets had several capital projects in their 2020–21 budget that would lay the groundwork for post-COVID-19 economic revival.

In September, the Commissioners Court adopted a county budget of $1.78 billion, holding to the current tax rate. Throughout the pandemic we continued to maintain our Triple-A rating from all three bond-rating agencies. We had frozen positions earlier, held off unnecessary spending, and were able to adopt a balanced budget that included funding for capital projects.

The Commissioners Court's budget included additional funding for the San Pedro Creek project, bringing our investment to over $200 million. The city included $20 million to pay for new bridges over the creek.

San Pedro Creek was being restored from a concrete drainage ditch back into a beautiful meandering creek passing through downtown. We had completed the first phase of the creek up to Houston Street, two blocks north of Plaza de Armas. The water quality and aquatic habitat was revitalized, and aquatic plants trees, shrubs, and grasses were planted. The history of Bexar County was told through 13 interpretive signs. Four different murals by local artists collectively spanned 114 ft. of the paseo. Nineteen tile benches were built along the pathway of the creek.

Prior to our media briefings, I enjoyed periodic walks along the creek, observing the work underway from Houston Street going south. Walking by myself gave me time to clear my mind and think about the future beyond COVID-19. Building for the future while struggling with the pandemic gave me hope.

As I walked along a high bank paseo on the west bank of the creek, I could see the newly created contours of the creek taking shape. The creek bed was widened, creating a meandering creek like it originally was. I passed by the beautifully designed limestone walls encompassing the creek and looked at the natural storm water filtration medium that was installed to clean water runoff. I could envision the lush landscaping and pedestrian lights that would come later.

Further south of Plaza de Armas, work was under way to reconstruct the bridges at Nueva and Graham Street that would allow pedestrian passage underneath the streets. It was estimated that we would complete the Nueva Street bridge in the spring of 2022, allowing the flow of water to begin. The lighting, plantings, and trees are to be installed by the summer 2022.

Several other projects were concurrently being built along the creek. The Alameda Theatre was being restored, and Texas Public Radio was constructing a new studio located in the same building. The federal courthouse was under construction, and apartments were being built along the creek. UTSA was constructing a new building, and the San Antonio Independent School

District was in the process of constructing a new administration building.

Completed section of the San Pedro Creek restoration.

While the county was working on restoring the creek, the city was reconstructing several downtown streets, restoring City Hall, and completing the remodeling of the Frost Tower that they had acquired. The most important city capital project was one in which they had a partnership with the Texas General Land Office to restore and expand the Alamo grounds where the famous Battle of the Alamo occurred in 1836. The project also included building a new museum where the Woolworth and Crockett buildings stood across from the plaza.

Work was underway on restoring the Alamo church and the Long Barrack and constructing a new exhibit building on the grounds behind the church. While I supported that work, I had opposed other elements of the plan that were in opposition to the plan that the City Council had approved on October 20, 1994, when I was mayor.

The current plan did not allow open pedestrian access to the plaza in front of the Alamo that had been a gathering place for citizens for decades. Instead, the plaza would be fenced off with one specific narrow point of entry that would be controlled. The plan also didn't allow parades in front of the Alamo, including the Battle of Flowers parade that commemorates the heroes of the Battle of the Alamo. It also did not protect the historic Woolworth building where the museum was envisioned.

On October 19, I had lunch with former San Antonio Mayor Phil Hardberger and Phil Bakke at Nicha's restaurant south of downtown across from Mission San Jose. While we were waiting for the waiter to serve us lunch, I answered a telephone call. I could not hear very well, so I walked outside to talk without my mask on. Someone took a picture of me, and it ended up on social media the next day. Bad mistake, and I admitted my failure to the media.

But that is not why I am telling the story of the lunch. I asked both Phils to join me in writing a letter to Mayor Nirenberg and the City Council supporting the three Alamo major principles that I had been advocating. I drafted the letter later, they approved it, and I sent it.

***

We began preparing for flu season. The good news was that all the commonsense COVID-19 safety measures were essentially the same to protect people from the flu. But most importantly, unlike COVID-19, we had a flu vaccine. We began advocating that everyone should get a flu shot.

On September 26, we partnered with UHS to give free flu shots at the Freeman Coliseum grounds. I watched as cars lined up to enter six different stations where the shots were being administered.

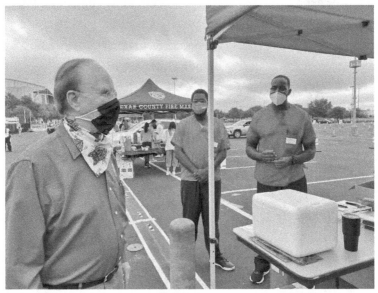

Bexar County, University Health, and H-E-B flu shot drive-thru held at Freeman Coliseum grounds on September 26, 2020.

We provided vaccines to 2,025 people that day and followed up with more events. Later Commissioners Sergio Rodriguez and Justin Rodriguez hosted flu vaccinations at other locations.

***

On October 2, I was surprised to hear that President Trump was admitted to Walter Reed National Medical Center with COVID-19. Surprised? I wondered why I felt that way. After all he made fun of face masks, had numerous events without anyone wearing them, and downplayed the COVID-19 threat for months.

He ended up staying three nights in the hospital where he was treated with remdesivir, an antiviral medication, and dexamethasone, a powerful anti-inflammatory drug. He was also treated with REGEN-COV, an experimental antibody cocktail that would eventually be approved by the FDA. He also was on supplemental oxygen on two occasions. By the way, he did not take chloroquine and hydroxychloroquine, the drugs he had recommended. Hospital staff also made sure that bleach was not within his reach.

Although there is no cure for COVID-19, the medicine he took was the best to prevent symptoms from getting worse. The rascal walked away from the hospital recovered and ready to campaign.

I thought the fact that COVID-19 almost put him down would change the attitude of Trump supporters and that they would begin to respond to health official's warnings. But they didn't. Instead, they looked at him as a hero who defeated COVID-19, and if he did, they could also.

***

Governor Abbott gave the green light to the Texas Alcohol Beverage Commission (TABC) to allow bars to open if they got a food permit or if a food truck parked near their bar. County judges were allowed to open small bars that could not afford to get a food permit or food truck to serve their customers.

I asked Metro Health to work with the health task force to make a recommendation. They advised that it was safe to open bars allowing only 50 percent capacity. I followed their recommendation and opened the few remaining bars on October 19 with the understanding that if a second COVID-19 wave came, they would have to close.

In the meantime, I felt very comfortable going to restaurants that were complying with health protocols. I believed that you were not likely to contract COVID-19 in a restaurant that complied with sanitation, face covering, and social distancing measures. If I were going to get COVID-19 it would be from anyone that went to lunch with me because we took off masks while sitting down and eating.

The restaurants had suffered the most throughout the pandemic, and I wanted to be part of their recovery. On our daily briefings I would state where I had lunch or dinner and what safety precautions they were taking. I mentioned Carmilitas, J. Alexanders, Jim's, Los Barrios, La Coronela, Tony G, Pam's, The Palm, La Paloma, Nicha's, Blanco Café, B & B Smoke House, Bill Miller Barbecue, Silos, Fredricks, and others.

I also spent time visiting our Bexar BiblioTech libraries, the nation's first all-digital public library. They proved to be an invaluable asset throughout the pandemic for those seeking information and books to read.

We opened the first BiblioTech library in 2013 on the south side, where 75 percent of the homes were not connected to the internet. Under the leadership of BiblioTech Administrator Laura Cole we built a 4,000 sq. ft. library that included study rooms, a children's area, and an open area that included 40 large-screen Apple Mac computers. We have a large collection of digital information, e-books, audiobooks, magazines, newspapers, and music along with free e-book readers and iPads.

Since then, Bexar County, with the financial support of the Hidalgo Foundation, has built three 4,000 sq. ft. libraries. All during the shutdown from March 13–May 5 we continued to provide curbside services for Wi-Fi hotspots, e-book readers, and iPads for people to check out. At the same time patrons who downloaded books over the internet increased substantially.

We reopened the BiblioTech libraries on May 5, limiting capacity to 25 percent, and instituted numerous safety measures such as requiring face masks, temperature checks, sanitation, and plexiglass guards at each computer station.

Traditional libraries were a problem to keep open during the pandemic because stacks and stacks of books are almost impossible to sanitize. But in a small paperless all-digital public library, it was easy to clean and sanitize.

During the pandemic we served thousands of patrons who came to pick up new e-book readers, download new books, and get WiFi hotspots and technical advice.

To date over 1.4 million people have visited our website. We now have over 200,000 e-books available. Patrons have checked out over one million e-books plus numerous other items such as magazines, movies, music, learning resources, and newspapers.

***

An extraordinary operation in October was performed at University Hospital by Dr. Edward Sako, the surgical director of the lung transplant program. Dr. Sako did a double lung transplant on COVID-19 patient Jose Sosa, age 39.

After spending time in a hospital in Corpus Christi, Sosa had been transferred to a San Antonio hospital. He did not improve, and doctors determined that his damaged lungs were beyond help. The double lung transplant was successfully accomplished, and he eventually went home. Sosa's case sent a message to people that even though a person may not die from COVID-19, serious illnesses can still result.

In early October we began preparations for the upcoming

presidential general election. We expected a huge turn out with the important presidential race between former Vice President Joe Biden and President Donald Trump. Never before had there been such a dramatic difference in political beliefs and character traits between two candidates.

Even though COVID-19 cases were under control we were concerned that the election could become a super spreader event and reignite a surge. Commissioner Justin Rodriguez took the lead in advocating proposals to make voting safer and easier. He proposed extending drive-thru voting, opening mega voting sites, keeping at least one poll station open for 24 hours during early voting, having at least 10 locations for dropping off ballots, and sending applications for paper ballots to all persons over 65 years of age.

The election policies adopted by the Commissioners Court led us into confrontation with the state. The attorney general prevailed in a lawsuit that prohibited poll stations from remaining open for 24 hours during early voting and eliminated the 10 locations we had proposed for dropping off mail ballots.

We established 48 early voting sites that included four mega sites, each with multiple voting stations. The large mega centers allowed us to prevent long lines and overcrowded conditions that could lead to the spread of COVID-19. We also set aside $6 million for protective screens, gloves, sanitation products, and other protective equipment.

On October 13 we got off to a strong start with 33,421 people voting the first day. Early voting would continue for 16 days. While voting was under way, Governor Abbott announced that the Texas National Guard would send 1,000 troops to the four major Texas cities to handle any disturbances, implying that he may use them at voting sites. No election officials had complained of disturbances. Nirenberg and I stated we were not informed of his decision and that it was totally unnecessary as our police and sheriff's departments could handle any problems.

While election voting was underway on October 21, for the first time, I gave my State of the County Address in an online format hosted by the San Antonio Chamber of Commerce. I focused on the economic recovery efforts we were taking.

While online meetings are ok, giving an online speech stinks. It seemed very strange talking to an audience but not being able to tell their reactions to what I was saying. There was no synergy and no follow up conversations after the speech. I was not sure what anybody thought of my remarks or if they were even listening.

The next day President Trump, during a presidential debate, said that the virus had vanished in Texas. That was good to know—if he said it, it must be true. Not hardly! He had been wrong about just about everything he had said about COVID-19.

Because the Commissioners Court had mailed early ballots and established mega centers for early voting, the majority of people had already voted before the November 3 election day. Voters sent in 92,589 mail ballots and 596,961 had voted early. Our early preparation to prevent the spread of COVID-19 and make it easy to vote early had prevented what could have been a very dangerous election.

Just before election day, positive COVID-19 infections moved up to 7.7 percent from an early October rate of 4.9. Prior to election day, we had provided our 900 election officials with free tests. On election day we provided protective equipment, sanitation, and personal safety clothing, but we could not require face masks because of the governor's emergency restrictions. We would eventually lose three election judges to COVID-19. Whether they contracted COVID-19 while working the elections, we will never know.

On Election Day, 84,246 voted, a small number compared to early voting and mail-in ballots. The election was an extraordinary effort by our election officials during a time of rising cases. The total vote of 770,566 was 30 percent higher than the previous record established in the 2016 presidential election year. We had a record turnout of 65 percent of eligible voters.

In his race for president, Joe Biden easily carried Bexar County with 58.20 percent to President Donald Trump's 40.05 percent, with the remaining votes going to third party candidates.

Trish DeBerry won her commissioner race with 54.60 percent and Rebeca Clay-Flores with 64.95 percent. It would be a new day as two new, very capable women were coming onto the court with a fresh perspective.

Election Day was an important day for Mayor Nirenberg. For over a year we had both been working on a public transit plan that would require a public vote to shift taxes away from aquifer protection and trail projects to public transit. Nirenberg promised that both programs would continue with a different funding source. But with the COVID-19 pandemic underway, Nirenberg changed his mind and wanted to secure additional funds for job training rather than public transit. I supported him.

However, VIA, our transit authority made up of city, county, and suburban appointees, held fast to calling their own election. Chairperson Hope Andrade was adamant about it.

Finally, Nirenberg reached an agreement with Andrade whereby the proposed sales tax could be used for four years to fund job training, then the remaining years the tax would go to public transit. During the first four years, $154 million would be made available to train as many as 40,000 workers.

In the meantime, Nirenberg secured a 10-year commitment from the City Council to fund aquifer protection. I had convinced the Commissioners Court to fund $240 million toward creek trail projects. These commitments helped hold down opposition to Nirenberg's plan.

Nirenberg organized and led the campaign. I joined his election night party where we saw the eye-popping returns giving him a 74 percent approval margin for work force and public transit. If anyone could ever turn a mandate into a successful upcoming May 2021 re-election mayoral campaign, Nirenberg now had the pathway—and he knew it.

After all the votes were counted nationwide, Biden defeated Trump 81,009,468 to 74,411,419. Biden received 306 electoral votes and Trump 232. I was surprised that Trump did as well as he did despite his erratic leadership throughout the pandemic. But Trump did not accept the election results and would, through November, December, and January, try whatever means necessary to overturn the election.

Three days after the election, my research aide James Rivera caught COVID-19. I was not around him much since only occasionally staff, as well as myself, came to the office. By now I was a frequent user of Zoom whose use went from ten million people a day in December 2019 to 300 million in June 2020. I discouraged in-person meetings. After learning of Rivera's positivity, I self-quarantined and had two tests that turned out negative.

Four days later Nirenberg announced that he would self-quarantine after being in contact with someone who later tested positive. Both of us were in good health and had been consistent in using face masks, so the risk was very low that we would get COVID-19.

On our November 9 briefing we reported that the positive

rate had gone up two weeks in a row, now up to 8.4 percent. Nirenberg called it a "significant jump in new cases." The CDC noted on the same day that the virus crisis was worsening, and that small household gatherings were an important contributor to spreading the virus.

As our hospitalized COVID-19 patients continued to rise, we also had to accept patients from El Paso, a city some 600 miles from San Antonio where a major outbreak had occurred. Located on the border of Mexico with the large Mexican city of Juarez on the other side, there was constant travel between the two cities that led to an explosion of cases. Their hospital system could not handle the influx of COVID-19 patients.

As a result, El Paso County Judge Ricardo Samaniego took the extraordinary step of shutting down businesses. His decision was quickly overruled by Governor Abbott. That is why Nirenberg and I were careful not to cause a confrontation with the governor if we thought we could not win. It only leads to the public becoming confused with two conflicting orders.

***

Since the implementation of our order in July requiring businesses to adopt health protocols including the requirement of face coverings, we had received great compliance. But now everybody was letting their guard down because they thought the pandemic was over.

Previously, in most cases if a business was not implementing the policy, we gave a warning and the business complied right away. Now with rising infections, we stopped giving warnings, and instead fines were accessed immediately.

Fines were accessed to 295 businesses. Follow-up visits were made, and additional fines accessed if they were not in compliance. If they refused to comply, the city moved to take away their certificate of occupancy. The first to be closed was XTC Cabaret.

Nirenberg stated on our show, "I have said numerous times, it is behavior—not specific locations—that continues the spread of the virus." He was absolutely right. Businesses that complied with safety precautions, including restaurants, were a safe environment.

Gatherings of people, including home family gatherings where people hang close together without masks, were the events Mr. COVID liked to attend. So, on November 20 we deployed an emergency alert to cell phones of residents urging people not to have Thanksgiving gatherings and to continue following health guidelines.

Prior to one of our evening briefings as Thanksgiving approached, Nirenberg asked me what I thought about a curfew over the Thanksgiving weekend. I responded that when college students came home, they would hang with their friends at bars and spread the virus. Nirenberg responded that he wanted to announce the curfew the day before the Thanksgiving weekend, in order to not allow time for the governor to overrule us.

We enacted the curfew, starting on Thanksgiving night at 10:00 a.m. to 5:00 a.m. Monday morning. A fine of $1,000 was imposed for violations. Officers responded to 63 calls for violations of the curfew, resulting in shutting down some bars.

Most restaurants were happy to comply, but many bar owners were not so happy. One bar owner did offer some defense for our order. He said early in the evening customers are quiet and respectful, but around 10:00 p.m. it starts getting a little loud and people start hugging up on each other, and after 10:00 p.m. the drinking increases and it gets pretty wild.

Besides bar owners, our order did not sit too well with the Trump crowd. About 100 of them gathered at the Alamo to protest. Later many of them went to the Angry Elephant bar, had a few drinks, and then headed for the neighborhoods where Mayor Nirenberg and I lived.

We live in neighborhoods across from each other. They drove down the street between our neighborhoods with flags flying, honking their horns. I thought that was pretty cool, a parade in our honor.

***

We opened a Regional Infusion Center on November 30 at the Bexar County Exposition Hall to administer the monoclonal antibody treatments to high-risk patients who were ill with COVID-19. The FDA had authorized the use of the monoclonal antibody therapy drugs bamlanivimab and estesevimab. The infusion drugs were for patients who were at a high risk of progressing to severe COVID-19 and having to enter the hospital. These antibody drugs cut the risk of hospitalization.

BCFS Health and Human Services, a non-profit institution led by director Kevin Dinnin, is based in San Antonio. They ran the Regional Infusion Center. The patients had to have tested positive, shown symptoms, and have a doctor's prescription. It takes about an hour for a transfusion, and its free.

We infused our first patient on December 1, 2020. Over the next three months the infusion center provided therapy to 3,008 patients. With the help of monoclonal antibody transfusions, fewer patients were becoming seriously ill. As a result, only 30 percent of our patients were in the ICU compared to 50 percent during the summer.

While we were making breakthroughs on COVID-19 medicine, and soon to be vaccines, we could have saved more lives if the state leadership had opted to expand Medicaid. Texas is the second worst state in the nation for health insurance coverage with nearly one-third of our citizens lacking coverage.

I stated at Commissioners Court that the state's failure to expand Medicaid led to numerous unnecessary deaths from COVID-19. Most of the COVID-19 patients that ended up in the hospital had underlying health conditions such as diabetes and heart conditions, and they had put off treatment because they did not have health insurance. Had they had proper medical treatment earlier many would not have ended up in the hospital.

Commissioners Court and City Council adopted resolutions urging the state to expand Medicaid and join the other 38 states who had adopted the expansion. Because of the COVID-19 crisis, we thought we finally had an opportunity to get the legislature to opt in. But sad to say we would not be successful in the next session of the legislature that would begin a month later in January.

By December 1, we had 593 COVID-19 patients in the hospital that had slowly grown from 227 on November 1. While we had seen a steady rise in hospitalizations, the cases were still manageable, but the steady rise indicated that it would get worse. We were optimistic that we would soon have vaccines. Pfizer's emergency request would go before the U.S. Food and Drug Administration on December 10. Moderna, like Pfizer, required two doses, and its request would be heard a week later.

While we were excited about possible FDA approval of vaccines, we realized it would take time to get two shots into everyone's arms and that would be impossible to achieve during the winter months. COVID-19 was picking up steam and could erupt into a surge as bad or worse than the summertime tsunami.

6. Wintertime Eruption, 2020–2021

UHS PRESIDENT GEORGE HERNANDEZ appeared before the Commissioners Court on December 1 to announce that they expected to be able to administer the vaccines to health care workers and first responders within about 10 days. It would take some time before the rest of the public could be vaccinated.

On that same day, the CDC shortened the length of quarantine time from 14 days to 10 days. If you then had a negative test, it was reduced to seven days. That was good news for businesses and a lot of people.

On December 6 our positivity rate jumped to 15.7 percent. From the increasing positivity rate, we knew more people would be entering the hospital since it takes a couple of weeks before infected people enter the hospital. Some entered the hospital and progressed to the ICU, then onto ventilators, and eventually died.

By now we had 576 COVID-19 patients in the hospital, of which 204 were in the ICU and 105 on ventilators. Numbers were growing each day just as they had in the summer that had eventually reached a high of 1,267 hospitalizations. We knew our patient load would grow and possibly reach the summer high. We also knew our current 1,397 COVID-19 deaths would rise.

Mayor Nirenberg began to make weekly pleas for citizens to donate to the South Texas Blood & Tissue Center, stressing the need for type O donors. It would continue to be a problem throughout the winter months.

On that same day Spurs coach Gregg Popovich smacked President Trump with a hard thrown basketball. He blasted the anti-mask Trump and referred to him as a "circus ringleader." It was an apt description of Trump, and we would soon see him assemble his carnies.

As we collected data, it became clear that the closeness and longevity of the contact with an infected person significantly increased the transmission of COVID-19. Local contact tracing found that 92 percent of infections were transmitted by close contact. That is why we continued to warn people not to gather, although we knew it would be very hard for them not to do so for Christmas. The Christmas season leads to New Year celebrations and that's a long time for Mr. COVID to dart around.

It would become a very dangerous time because we saw the resulting rise in cases after Thanksgiving. While it was not a large spike, partially because we had imposed a curfew, we knew that with the upcoming long Christmas holiday season, we could not get away with another curfew.

On our December 10 media briefing we revealed a letter that we wrote to the governor requesting that teachers be added to the priority list for vaccinations. They were on the front line teaching our children. This led to a group of teachers in Alamo Heights getting together to make yard signs that stated, "Nirenberg, Wolff and Teachers." It was a very nice tribute and we thanked them.

We received our first batch of vaccines at University Hospital on December 14. The effort to produce the vaccine by the pharmaceutical industry and virus research labs was incredible. They had developed the vaccine five times faster than any other in history. And that was possible because it was different than any vaccine they had developed in the past.

Since the mid-1880s vaccines were given by injecting a weakened and safe form of an infectious disease that activates your immune system to develop antibodies to recognize and fight the dangerous agent. We have used these types of vaccines to fight off measles, mumps, rubella, and chicken pox.

We used this approach because we were not as smart as bacteria. Bacteria are single-celled organisms lacking a distinct nucleus that have fought off viruses for over a billion years. Over time, bacteria develop cluster repeated sequences that can remember and destroy the virus. Their immune system adapts itself to ward off new waves of viruses.

Humans are complex organisms made up of trillions of cells, each with its own structure and function. We have about 200 different types of cells. They are the building blocks of all living things; they take in nutrients from food and convert the nutrients into energy as well as carrying out specialized functions. They also contain the body's hereditary material and can make copies of themselves. Thus, it is much more difficult to develop cluster repeated sequences that remember and destroy viruses for our complex cells.

I had the opportunity to read Walter Isaacson's book, *Code Breaker*, and became fascinated with the science researchers who had developed a tool, known as CRISPR, to edit DNA. Biologists learned how to use CRISPR to edit human DNA by using RNA as a messenger. The DNA molecule is composed of two polynucleotide chains coiled around each other to form a double helix and is the repository of genetic information. The RNA molecules are nucleic acids that are associated with the control of cellular chemical activities. RNA oversees the making of proteins and acts as a guide for enzymes.

The idea and work on an mRNA vaccine began in the early '80s, long before CRISPR. So, this technology helped advance the concept, but the work of people on mRNA vaccines largely doesn't intersect with CRISPR work.

Biologists developed a genetic vaccine by injecting a snippet of RNA (mRNA) into humans that will guide human cells to produce components of the virus that will in turn stimulate the immune system. The RNA instructs cells to make part of a spike protein that is on the surface of coronavirus that gives our cells instructions on how to fight COVID-19. The RNA does its work in the outer regions of the cells and does not need to get into the nucleus or change anything about our own DNA. The piece of spike protein created from the vaccine allows our bodies to create memories to recognize COVID-19 and kill it as soon as it tries to attack us—brilliant move.

In 2020 both Moderna and Pfizer-BioNTech used this approach and were approved for emergency use. After the vaccines proved to be 90 percent effective, many scientists felt that we were ushering in a golden age of vaccinology.

Four days after receiving our vaccines at University Hospital, I asked Mayor Nirenberg to meet me at the hospital to observe how the vaccine was handled and administered.

It was cold as I walked through the huge, elongated portico in front of the hospital, much like the cold, windy day of March 2014 when we held the grand opening ceremonies under the portico. I was proud of the Commissioners Court for providing funding for the new 10-story hospital, located in the South Texas Medical Center on the northwest side of San Antonio.

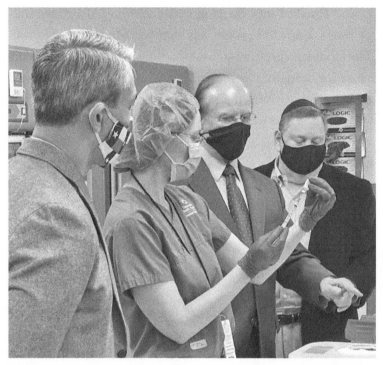

Vaccine Briefing at University Hospital on December 18, 2020, where Judge Wolff and Mayor Nirenberg are shown first-hand the process for preparing and administering the COVID-19 vaccine.

The hospital has 420 new private rooms, an interactive entertainment/patient education system, 35 surgical suites, including state-of-the-art technology, a new electronic medical records system, an expanded emergency center, and an AirLIFE helipad on top of the hospital.

Now six years later, the hospital still looked stunning with its sheets of glass alternating with colors of blue, white, and transparent patterned to resemble the sky. I glanced at the opposite wall of the portico where local artist Riley Robinson had painted thousands of bluebonnets, the state flower of Texas.

I walked into the large lobby surrounded by outstanding works of art. To the right was a net-like sculpture dotted with colorful disks representing foxglove, the plant that produced the life-saving heart drug. To the left, a series of crimson plates showed the face of Hippocrates, the father of western medicine. Above was an expanse of glass with strands of color representing DNA.

Throughout the hospital we had approved more than 1,000 original works of art and design enhancements. According to the Department of Health's Working Group on Arts and Health, art is healing and results in shorter hospital stays, less medication, and fewer complications. Art also improves workplace satisfaction and reduces anxiety.

I took the elevator up to the second floor where I joined President George Hernandez, Chief of Pharmacy Elliot Mandell, and Mayor Nirenberg. It was fascinating to watch the intricate process that must be implemented to store and use the vaccine. A pharmacist reached into the freezer where the vaccine was kept at −80 degrees centigrade for as long as six months. She had three minutes to close the door.

She removed a batch of tiny capsules and placed it in a refrigerator next to the freezer where they could thaw out. It could only remain in the refrigerator up to five days. It was then thawed out at room temperature for one hour.

Once thawed, a precise amount of saline must be added to dilute the vaccine within a two-hour window. Six doses of diluted vaccine per vial was injected into individual syringes. Each syringe was labeled with an expiration time and a bar code and then loaded into an Epic electronic medical record. At this point the vaccine had to be administered within six hours.

The syringes were then handed off to a nurse who proceeded to an adjoining room where shots would be given to the staff of University Hospital. We watched them give the shots and then visited with a few of those who had received their first dose while they waited for the required 15 minutes to see if they had a reaction. No one had a reaction, although some said their arms were sore, a common side effect after receiving the vaccine.

As we began vaccinating health care workers, people began to call asking when it would be available to them. We stated on our December 16 briefing that it was up to the governor to determine who would first be eligible after health care workers were vaccinated. The state would issue us a weekly supply of vaccines, and we would face a logistical nightmare when the time came to vaccinate the over two million people who lived in Bexar County.

On our December 21 public briefing, Dr. Rita Espinoza, Metro Health Chief Epidemiologist, stated that we would probably see six to eight weeks of increased infections, depending on how individuals took precautions. We knew young people were not being cautious.

I pointed out that those in their 20s accounted for 21.5 percent of COVID-19-infected people, but they were only 15 percent of the population. I went on to say that while they may not get sick, they would bring it home to their parents, grandparents, and other older people perhaps causing them to have a very serious illness.

Nirenberg stated on our December 23 media briefing that we had 912 COVID-19 patients in the hospital, with 292 in the ICU and 145 on ventilators. I said based on our model we could reach a height of 1,700 patients which would push our hospital capacity to the limit.

***

During December I had several conversations with San Antonio Livestock Exposition (SALE) Chairperson Nancy Loeffler. I told her it could be a dangerous to hold the rodeo in February, depending on how long the winter surge of COVID-19 would last.

SALE has a longer history in San Antonio than the Spurs. In 1950, they began holding their rodeo in the Freeman Coliseum that the county had built on 184 acres of Bexar County property. When we opened the new county arena in 2003, SALE began having their rodeo in the new facility where the Spurs play. In the new arena they substantially increased their revenue and were able to attract talented performers. They have been recognized every year since as the best indoor rodeo in the nation.

SALE has a lease on the 184-acre grounds, the arena, the Coliseum, and Exposition Hall during the 17 days of the rodeo. Under the lease they have full control over their events, subject to health guidelines set by the state.

Throughout December I was able to work with Chairperson Loeffler to have a scaled-down version of the rodeo. Under the direction of CEO Cody Davenport, they moved the rodeo from the 18,000-seat capacity of the arena to the smaller Coliseum and reduced capacity to 40 percent of the 10,000-seat capacity. They also reduced their outdoor events, holding total attendance down to about 120,000 from a normal attendance of 1.5 million people. Temperature checks and face masks would be required.

I also reached an agreement with them to cancel the carnival which typically draws the most people. The Commissioners Court also had provided $750,000 to the rodeo to help make up the losses of canceling the carnival.

In addition to the precautions that the rodeo would take, the Commissioners Court had invested over $5 million to add public health features to the Coliseum, county arena, and expo halls. They included touchless restroom fixtures, antiviral lighting, enhanced ventilation, and contact-free payment options.

I was happy about the safer and scaled down event, but I still thought they should delay the rodeo. The Houston Livestock Show and Rodeo and the Fort Worth Stock Show had been postponed. I would continue to ask SALE to reconsider.

***

It was a strange, lonely Christmas Day for Tracy and me, as it was for many families. The only family member we saw over the Christmas season was Tracy's son Paul Wendland and his 14-year-old stepson Ben. They came over on Christmas morning and we shared gifts, and then Tracy prepared dinner. We checked in with the rest of our children and grandchildren over Zoom.

Two days after Christmas President Trump signed an additional $900 million pandemic relief bill. It established a $300 per week supplemental jobless benefit and a $600 direct stimulus payment. It would be a financial savior for people out of a job.

After the Texas Department of State Health Services announced in December that Texans who are 65 years and older were eligible for the COVID-19 vaccine, Tracy and I decided that we should set an example by agreeing to be vaccinated. Many people were leery about the vaccine due to the fast-track development. At the time Tracy was 77 and I was 80.

On December 30 we went to University Hospital to get our shots. A picture was taken, and it ended up on the front page of the *San Antonio Express-News*. Both of us had sore arms. While Tracy did not have any other reaction, I did experience a slight headache that night, but that was all.

When we got our shots I talked with President George Hernandez, and he told me they were planning to administer shots at Wonderland Mall where they had a clinic that would open on January 4. People would have to call and make an appointment.

On December 31 Trump delivered a year-end video message calling the vaccine a "truly unprecedented medical miracle" and said it would be available to every American early this coming year. This would prove to be the major accomplishment of the Trump administration, but unfortunately as the vaccine became available many of his supporters would become anti-vaccine advocates, better known as "anti-vaxxers."

We ended the year with 1,122 COVID-19 patients in the hospital, of which 314 were in ICU and 170 on ventilators. It was a sad ending to 2020 for families with stricken family members. By now the pandemic had taken 1,402 lives of our citizens in Bexar County.

Normally on New Year's Eve the city would host a major event downtown featuring singers, food, and fireworks. But this year it would be an event hosted by Bexar County and San Antonio Parks Foundation that would be watched on television. We set off a dazzling firework show along with music that lasted 12 minutes.

With the start of the new year, we knew the winter surge of COVID-19 would only get worse. It would be a horrible way to greet the new year, but at the same time we looked forward to finally conquering COVID-19 with a successful vaccination campaign.

Mayor Nirenberg and I took a tour of the opening of the Wonderland mass vaccine site on January 4. After we passed and greeted several people in line to get their shots, we were met by President Hernandez, Executive Vice President Leni Kirkman, and Senior Vice President Bill Phillips.

First day of UHS mass vaccination site at Wonderland Mall on January 4, 2021. Judge Wolff greets people in line waiting to receive the vaccine.

We watched as people checked in, having to show some identification, and then were escorted to one of six stations where nurses administered the shots. We had a waiting room where they were required to remain for 15 minutes after taking the shot so they could be monitored for possible adverse reactions.

While the work was intense at the mall there was also additional work to be done before the vaccines arrived at the mall. Pharmacists started the day at 4:00 a.m. at University Hospital where they picked up the thawed vitals of the undiluted vaccine for the people who had registered for an appointment. The pharmacist at the mall diluted the medication with saline and then drew up individual doses. They were ready at 8:00 a.m. to begin administering the doses. Any extra doses were given at the end of the evening for people without appointments. We vaccinated 1,400 people with the Moderna vaccine on our first day.

We also provided vaccinations at our new downtown six-story clinical facility located on our Robert B. Green campus. With funding from the Commissioners Court, the six-story brick building was built and opened on January 13, 2013. Like the new hospital in the medical center, it includes sculptures and paintings throughout the building. The building includes 162 examination rooms and 21 advanced treatment rooms. The clinic has the best of equipment, including two new MRI scans and six new CT scans.

On January 5, University Hospital Chief Medical Officer Dr. Bryan Alsip joined us on our briefing show. Because of the high number of COVID-19 patients in the hospital, Alsip announced that they were postponing elective surgeries to preserve beds like the hospitals had to do the previous summer. They would continue performing procedures for severe and life-threatening conditions.

As we were struggling through the winter COVID-19 surge, on January 6 we witnessed an unprecedented attack on the United States Capitol. Our democracy came under attack as the "circus ringleader" (as defined by Spurs Coach Popovich), rounded up his carnies to march on the Capitol to stop the certification of the presidential election results by Congress. Trump demanded that Vice President Mike Pence and Congress reject Biden's victory.

At noon, at a "Save America" rally on the Ellipse, Trump said, "If you don't fight like hell, you're not going to have a country anymore." After the rally, the crowd headed toward the Capitol, breaching police perimeters and breaking in. Some shouted,

"Hang Mike Pence." They looted the office of Speaker Nancy Pelosi and ransacked the empty Senate Chamber. The House and Senate members were sequestered in a safe area just in time.

Finally, after President-elect Joe Biden asked Trump to call off his supporters, Trump did so at 4:17 p.m., four hours after the melee began. Many in the crowd were armed and several had handguns that police later seized. In one rioter's pickup, parked next to the Capitol, police found weapons including a handgun, a rifle, and a shotgun along with hundreds of rounds of ammunition. They also found a large capacity ammunition feeding device. Five people died and 140 were injured. Over 600 people were arrested and charged with crimes. Damage to the Capitol was estimated to be $1.5 million.

Later that night, after the capitol grounds were cleared, the counting of the electoral votes continued and concluded the next morning. Pence declared Joe Biden and Kamala Harris elected as President and Vice President. He affirmed they would assume office on January 20, 2021.

If Vice President Pence, Senator Majority Leader Mitch McConnell, and a handful of Republicans had not joined Democrats to stand up to Trump, our democracy would have tumbled into oblivion.

The following day Facebook banned Trump from using its platform, Instagram barred Trump from posting, and Snapchat suspended Trump's account, followed by Twitch and Twitter.

Trump would be impeached again in February, but again it was a waste of time. Trump remained as popular as ever with his supporters and would go on to continue being the major force within the Republican Party. In fact, he would dominate the GOP. Ironically the very next day after the Trump-inspired riot, we saw the highest count of people in our hospitals since summer. We now had 1,341 in the hospital, which exceeded our summer record of 1,267 patients on July 13.

On January 8 the city opened a mass vaccination site at the Alamodome, a huge facility that was built and opened on May 15, 1993, when I was mayor. It has 165,000 square feet of exhibit space, 30,000 square feet of meeting rooms, and can seat 65,000. Over the years it has played host to football, basketball, soccer, boxing, and baseball games as well numerous other entertainment events and graduations.

Mayor Nirenberg, State Senator Jose Menendez, Commissioner Rebeca Clay-Flores, Representative Barbara Gervin-Hawkins, and I attended the opening. We walked up the outside steps to enter the southern entrance of the dome and were greeted by at the registration desks. We then walked along where numerous vaccination stations were positioned.

Judge Wolff, Mayor Nirenberg, Commissioner Rebeca Clay-Flores, and Rep. Barbara Gervin-Hawkins at the city's Alamodome mass vaccination site on January 11, 2021.

The setting was a little difficult, so the city also offered a drive-thru option that most peopled opted for. Along with our mass vaccination site at Wonderland, we were now able to move quickly on getting shots into arms.

Frustration continued to grow when people could not get an appointment because we only had a limited number of vaccines allocated to us by the state. Mayor Nirenberg and I sent a letter to the governor requesting more vaccines, but it would take time for the industry to produce and deliver enough.

***

On January 10, I lost my very best friend Glynn Dyess to COVID-19. We had remained close friends for 65 years. We first met at Pershing Jr. High School in Houston, Texas, in 1956. We became fast friends playing football for Pershing. We then attended Bellaire High School.

Wearing rolled up jeans, loafers, white t-shirts, and red jackets, we fancied ourselves as James Dean lookalikes from *Rebel Without a Cause*. We lived a carefree high school life, playing sports, chasing girls, and learning by osmosis. One day my counselor said I was performing well below my IQ—I was glad he saw the potential.

We played on the Bellaire football and baseball team, where Glynn was by far the best player. In our senior year, 1959, our football record was 8–2 and we won the city championship in baseball. We were also officers in the Bellaire Varsity Club, no doubt our highest academic record, if you could call it that.

In my senior year my dad said to go to the Mercury dealership and pick a car out for myself. Glynn went with me, and we chose a 1959 orange Mercury with a 290-horsepower V8 engine.

The Mercury became a much cooler car after my brother George put tail pipes along each side of the car and hung large Styrofoam dice over the rear-view mirror.

After coming back home to San Antonio, Glynn and I remained friends. Glynn would go on to start a successful oil pipeline business and make tons of money. We would ski together, go to Astros games, catch some NFL games, and dine at Toney's, Glynn's favorite restaurant.

A political life, because of its volatility, leads to a life of broken friendships—but not so with Glynn. Even though he was a very conservative Republican, he continued to support me knowing that my political beliefs were much different than his. He was one of my largest contributors in my various campaigns.

His wife Connie desperately wanted to be with him after he was taken to hospital with COVID-19, but due to the danger of transmission she was not allowed. Connie and I would talk each day.

Then at 6:15 p.m. on Sunday, January 10, she learned he had passed away after a nurse called to tell her a little red light went off at the nurse's station. He died alone, a terrible, horrifying way to die. The following night, on January 11, I told my story during our daily briefing show. I choked up and concluded by saying how difficult it was for Connie and me not being able to be with him and how horrible it was to die alone like so many other COVID-19-stricken patients had.

I later spoke at his funeral and concluded by saying I did not get to say goodbye to my best friend of 65 years. I knew it was a final parting, but it is a friendship I will always carry with me until my time comes.

***

In the midst of the pandemic our criminal justice system was struggling to keep up with cases. We were unable to hold jury trials, causing a long deferral in many cases. By late December we had a backlog of cases including those seeking protective orders related to domestic violence. Being home too long during the pandemic had led to family confrontations.

The Commissioners Court provided $350,000 to hire three prosecutors and a paralegal to handle protective orders. We also provided an additional $492,000 to the 14 courts to handle family violence cases.

On January 13 we reported the second highest single day of deaths since the pandemic began. We lost 25 of our citizens to COVID-19, bringing our death toll since the pandemic began to 1,685. We would see our death count double over the next three months.

Usually once a week I would have one of the commissioners take my place on the show. I thought it was good for citizens to see and hear a fresh perspective from the commissioners.

Commissioner Tommy Calvert appeared on our media briefing on January 18 and announced that he previously had COVID-19, had quarantined for 14 days, and had lost his taste. He said, "I hadn't cooked for a while, but I did not think my food would be so bland."

Calvert had notified us earlier of his case and attended our court meeting through Zoom. All through the pandemic the Commissioners Court had continued to meet in person. We were able to do so because Tracy and I had led an effort to restore the historic courtroom to its original large size. Tracy began raising money as a match to the Commissioners Court funding.

We had removed a floor that was installed in 1967 to split

the courtroom in two. Large wood-framed windows were made visible, stretching 25 feet up to the ceiling. We rebuilt the balcony that included 75 seats. The original 13 rose windows, replicas of the famous rose window at Mission San Jose, had been covered up with plaster and were now revealed in all their glory. The original plaster crown moldings and low-relief coffering was restored. We held our grand opening of the restored courtroom on January 6, 2015.

With our large courtroom we were able to spread out our five court members on temporary desks six feet apart. We limited attendance in the courtroom to only a few people at a time. Everyone was required to wear masks.

Commissioners Court first meeting on Januray 15, 2021, with two new commissioners. Left to right, Commissioner Rebeca Clay-Flores, Justin Rodriguez, Nelson Wolff, Trish DeBerry, and Tommy Calvert.

By January 18 we hit a high of 1,520 COVID-19 patients in the hospital, accounting for 36.6 percent of all hospital patients. Most disturbing was that for the first time we had 437 patients in the ICU and 260 on ventilators.

The following night in our media briefing I announced that since the pandemic started a total of nearly 5,600 COVID-19 patients had been hospitalized through the end of 2020. I thought this information might alert citizens to the magnitude of the pandemic. Nirenberg reminded people each number was a loved one who had suffered, causing pain and sadness to those who loved them.

I stated our data showed that 92 percent of infected people who claimed they knew where they were when they got infected said it came from an infected person at home. With young people being the greatest carriers, they were in many cases bringing it home to mom and dad—like the 22-year-old son of Graham Weston.

On the same day we had a virtual ground-breaking for the new UTSA School of Data Science and National Security Collaboration Center located downtown on San Pedro Creek. UTSA President Taylor Eighmy had secured the funding from the University of Texas Board of Regents and chose to build it downtown.

The city had contributed the land to UTSA to construct a six-story 165,000 sq. ft. building that would house classrooms, laboratories, and innovative space along with a café. Over 70 faculty members would teach cybersecurity, cloud computing, data and analytics, and artificial intelligence; the center would also provide government, industry, and community partners access to these programs. It would draw up to 6,500 students downtown.

Individually participants in the groundbreaking would go over to the site to be recorded. It was located on the eastern side of San Pedro Creek and faced Nueva. Across the street the Federal Courthouse was being built.

As I stood on the site talking about the significance of the new building, I pointed across the creek to where we were in the process of taking down a ten-story jail that had housed 600 federal pretrial inmates since 1987. When finished, Bexar County would provide the 2.6-acre site to UTSA to build a $161 million, 250,000 sq. ft. Innovation, Entrepreneurship and Careers Building.

***

Tracy and I received our second dose of the Pfizer vaccine on January 20, 2021. On that same day, we held a press conference to announce that we were ready to vaccinate school personnel in nine local school districts. University Hospital began registering them that day and would administer the shots at our Wonderland Mall mass vaccination site. Nirenberg and I were happy that our efforts to get schoolteachers and staff vaccinated was now underway.

Nelson and Tracy Wolff receive their second vaccine shot.

By the end of January our positive cases reached a total of 169,688 and 2,060 people had died. The magnitude of the winter COVID-19 surge resulted in 600 deaths in January alone, 150 more deaths than the previous high for any one month.

On February 2 Mayor Nirenberg announced for re-election over a virtual event live-streamed over Facebook. I wholeheartedly endorsed him this time and cut a media spot for him. Over the year of the pandemic, we had grown close as we worked together to control the spread of COVID-19. I was impressed with his leadership.

Nirenberg's opponent Greg Brockhouse, who in the previous race came close to defeating him, was coming back for a second try. But he would be facing a different Nirenberg. Nirenberg had not only provided strong leadership in the pandemic, he had also won a great victory in passing his job training program in the November election.

***

In early February, I received a call from former Bexar County Judge Cyndi Taylor Krier, who had supported my appointment to take her place after she resigned to become a regent of the University of Texas System in May 2001. We have remained friends over the last 20 years that I have served as county judge.

She told me that she was serving as Co-Chair of the NCAA Women's Final Four basketball championship. Rather than having the Final Four in San Antonio in April, because of the COVID-19 pandemic the NCAA was now considering several cities where they would bring 64 tournament teams to play 63 games over 15 days. By having all the post-season tournaments in one location they would be able to adapt better health safety measures. Cyndi believed they were going to be successful, and she wanted my support.

I responded that I wanted to hear about the COVID-19 protocols. She told me the plan was no fans at most games and for people to be socially distanced and masked in the Alamodome final rounds. Players would be in a restricted bubble at the hotels. No fans or family members would be allowed in the team hotels. Those seemed like strong protocols, so I decided to support her.

Cyndi also mentioned that ESPN would be broadcasting all 63 games nationwide, and the NCAA would buyout seven hotels and coordinate with other hotels for thousands of rooms. They would use a total of 20,000 rooms. This would be great for our hotel industry and restaurants that needed help. Unlike the rodeo that would be held in February, the Women's Final Four would be held in late March and April.

Nirenberg had been working behind the scenes to attract the event. On February 5, I publicly said I supported the games and that I thought we would get them. A few days later they announced they were coming. Nirenberg and I were both thrilled as it would be a great shot in the arm for our reeling hospitality and tourism industry.

The tournament proved to be a great success and had a $27.2 million economic impact. Most importantly, all safety protocols were followed, which prevented any increase in COVID-19 cases.

***

On February 11, it was announced that an arctic blast was heading our way with temperatures dipping into single digits. We assembled our public works teams and were ready to de-ice roadways and closed overpasses, assemble a rescue team, and provide warm places for those who needed them. But this storm would have another dimension that the State of Texas, CPS Energy, and the San Antonio Water System (SAWS) were not prepared for.

The next day Governor Abbott issued a disaster declaration stating that the weather posed an imminent threat of widespread and severe property damage, injury, and loss of life. The winter storm was caused by a disruption of the polar vortex, and the storm was potentially historic. The polar vortex is a swirling mass of cold air that circulates 10 to 30 miles above the artic trapping cold air. With artic temperatures increasing, some meteorologists believe that the warming air may affect the periodic break-up of the polar vortex and send blasts of cold air deeper into the United States.

After reading the governor's statement, I wondered if our community, for the first time, would experience the detrimental effects of climate change in an unprecedented way. Greenhouse gas emissions involve more than just temperatures. It changes precipitation like rain and snow, and the weather may become more extreme.

Numerous studies have shown that climate change has also led to the spread of infectious diseases. The extremes of heat and cold patterns, drought, flooding, and deforestation lead to increased migration of animals and connection between new groups of animals and humans. This can facilitate the transmission of viruses from one animal to another and to humans.

I wondered if climate change was also leading to the spread of the COVID-19 virus. While there was no definitive study of a connection between climate change and COVID-19, a later study would later find possible links between climate change and the transmission of COVID-19 through bats who had migrated because of climate change.

On Saturday, February 13, Nirenberg and I issued a joint declaration urging residents to take precautions ahead of the storm. We encouraged people to stay at home.

On Sunday, the Electric Reliability Council of Texas (ER-COT) issued a conservation alert to Texans asking consumers and businesses to reduce their electricity use as much as possible from Sunday through Tuesday. CPS Energy also asked customers to reduce electrical and natural gas use.

At about 10:00 p.m. Sunday night, I looked out the window and saw snow falling as the temperature fell to about 13 degrees. I felt like a kid going to bed, anxious to wake up the next morning and play in a rare snow.

On Monday morning, February 15, I woke up to a beautiful clear blue sky with snow covering our courtyard, giving it a white purity that I had not seen since 1985, the last time San Antonio had enough snow to cover the ground for a few days. I was excited and bundled up and started walking through the neighborhood.

As I walked, I was careful not to step on car tracks where ice lay exposed. It was a beautiful sight in the neighborhood as trees featured snowflakes and grass peeked out from the snow. A nice top of snow was on outdoor furniture and roofs throughout the neighborhood.

Later that same day, ERCOT required CPS Energy to participate in a statewide coordinated effort to cut power to consumers. That meant that the Texas electrical system could crash if demand was not cut back. Many electrical and gas suppliers had gone offline due to their equipment freezing. Later that night, the temperature fell to nine degrees.

On Tuesday, February 16, our electricity went off as CPS began rolling blackouts. CPS officials said the outage would only last 10 to 15 minutes but in fact it lasted for hours. Many citizens, including Tracy and me, were only getting electricity for about for five minutes at a time.

We were one household out of 372,000 households without power for long periods of time. Nirenberg and his wife Erika Prosper had also lost power to their home, so he used a cellular connection to conduct press briefings via WebEx to give the public updates on storm impacts, outages, and assistance that was available. The city and county provided shelter in hotels, motels, and the convention center for those seeking a warm place.

I went to H-E-B and Walmart that day seeking groceries, flashlights, batteries, and candles. At Walmart I had to stand in line outside for a half hour, giving my little toes a frosty reception. I also went to our vaccination site at Wonderland Mall. University Hospital kept the site open on reduced hours for people who were determined to get their shots. There was a good-sized turnout with over 1,000 people who were happy to see us open.

Throughout the storm we continued to vaccinate people at Wonderland Mall. Had we closed, the backup of citizens wanting shots would have exploded.

UHS health officials vaccinating people on February 9 at the Wonderland mass vaccination site.

Then on Wednesday, February 17, 60 of the 80 San Antonio Water System's plants shut down because CPS had also cut off electrical power to several pumping stations that were not on uninterruptible critical circuits. How smart was this? Now we had two emergencies.

Many citizens, including Tracy and me, lost their water supply. Tracy was smart enough to fill our bathtub with water before it was cut off. SAWS announced that as a safety measure, people should boil their water. We had a gas cooktop, so we took their advice, but many homes only had electricity and were unable to sanitize their water.

On Thursday, February 18 the snowfall lasted almost all day long. It wasn't as much fun as it was on Monday when I took a walk in the snow. Nirenberg and I returned to our daily COVID-19 briefing show via WebEx after an absence of three days during the worst part of the storm. Half the briefing focused on the COVID-19 emergency and half on updates on storm recovery efforts.

On Saturday, February 19 as the weather started warming, electricity and water were restored. But people's water pipes started busting all over town as ours did in the garage. The city and county appropriated funds to help citizens with plumbing repairs.

But all was not bad. No television gave us more time to read books by candlelight. We got used to wearing three layers of clothing in the house and covering up with multiple blankets. It was kind of nice to snuggle up.

Mr. Freeze caused Mr. COVID to slow down because people followed the mantra, "Stay Home, Work Safe." By February 21 we were down to 595 patients in the hospital, a drop of 206 since we got the storm warning 10 days earlier. Mr. Freeze also impacted the rodeo as most people chose not to attend, and thereby the threat of a super-spreader event was gone.

A later report from a committee that Mayor Nirenberg had appointed and chaired by former Councilman Reed Williams found that most of the problem lay with the state who had failed to regulate gas and electrical suppliers. It was not profitable for private companies to winterize their facilities, so they didn't do so with a great cost to the citizens of our state. The next session of the legislature passed legislation that ordered electrical and gas suppliers to winterize their facilities. But it lacked teeth, and those that chose to do so would take years to accomplish.

The report found that CPS Energy and SAWS failed in providing information to the public and to the Emergency Operations Center. CPS Energy failed to adequately winterize their power plants, and their roll out of cutting electrical power was chaotic. SAWS did not provide stand-by generators for their pumping stations. While we focused on the failures of the state and CPS, I hope all of us understand that climate change is our real problem. We are all culprits in destroying our planet with greenhouse gas emissions that lead to abrupt climate changes and foster the spread of infectious diseases.

***

While health officials and academia had collected data on COVID-19, it was unexpected that the NFL would provide even better information. In early February the NFL released data that they had compiled during their 256-game season. They had played before very limited crowds and had imposed several COVID-19 safeguards for the players and staff. They had conducted 954,830 tests on more than 7,000 people a week and had confirmed 724 cases, resulting in several players and staff having to be quarantined.

Before their data was released, public health officials had said that in most cases you had to be within six feet of someone for around 15 minutes to contact COVID-19. The NFL data revealed players became infected after being around a carrier far less than 15 minutes and further apart than six feet. It also revealed that when you were around a person inside who had COVID-19 and were unmasked you could become infected regardless of the time around an infected person. Nirenberg and I shared this new data with our citizens.

∗∗∗

By the end of February, we were down to 447 COVID-19 patients in the hospital from a high of 1,520 patients on January 18. The curve was going down at roughly the same slope as the downward summer surge, indicating that we would we continue to see COVID-19 retreating.

We had managed our way through the summer surge of 2020 and now were on the downside of the winter surge. After two battles maybe this time the war was over and Mr. COVID-19 had been licked. But then again, he may have something else up his sleeve.

The longer a virus continues to spread the more likely it will mutate and perhaps emerge into an enhanced version of its former self—kind of like Clark Kent turning into Superman. In December, there was a new variant spreading in India, but at the time there was no evidence it was any more dangerous. So, when flowers began to bloom in early March, we had no reason to suspect an enhanced mutation.

Spring is a renewable time when life springs back for all animals, including us. The vaccination miracle was renewing us, putting in place a defensive mechanism to ward off COVID-19. But it would take time to get everyone vaccinated, and we had to overcome the anti-vaccination crowd.

7. Springtime Renewal

ON MARCH 2, 2021, GOVERNOR Abbott lifted all COVID-19 restrictions and opened Texas 100 percent. All businesses could operate at full capacity without any mandatory health safety. His announcement was, in effect, a premature victory statement. Unlike his announcement in May 2020 that opened most businesses and lifted mandatory health safety requirements but kept schools closed, this time everything was off the table.

At our media briefing Nirenberg said, "You don't cut off your parachute just as you're slowing your descent." I stated that we were still going to see more people getting sick and dying, and that would prove to be true.

We still had 418 COVID-19 patients in the hospital and more were entering each day. A month later we reported 480 more deaths during March, bringing our total to 3,150 COVID-19 deaths. Abbott's order also caused confusion at numerous businesses. They had been enforcing our emergency mandate that required they adopt safety measures, including wearing face coverings. Without our mandate they had to decide to drop the mask mandate or keep one in place. Each business went their own way, making customers mad at them either way they went.

In March a new Bexar Fact's poll was revealed. Nirenberg and I were still maintaining our high approval rating, but Abbott's rating fell from 61 percent to 45 percent. His stripping away of health safety protocols that led to summer and winter COVID-19 surges drove his approval rating down.

I did get a bit of good news on the same day of Abbott's new order opening up Texas. I thanked Nirenberg that night at our media briefing when he said he supported a revised Alamo plan. This plan would leave Alamo Plaza open to pedestrians and special parades, such as the Battle of Flowers, and save the historic Woolworth and Crocket buildings and repurpose them into the Alamo Museum.

Nine days later the *San Antonio Express-News* published an article penned by Hardberger, Bakke, and me. We called upon the City Council to support the revised plan. Three days later, on April 15, Hardberger and I appeared before the council to support the new Alamo plan. The vote was ten-to-one in favor of the revisions.

Finally, the second battle of the Alamo was over when Texas Land Commissioner George P. Bush and Lieutenant Governor Dan Patrick announced their support of the revised plan the next day.

***

With our mandatory safety measures tossed aside by the governor, we concentrated on increasing vaccinations. On March 23, I announced that UHS had a record week, vaccinating 31,202 in one week at the Wonderland Mall. We now had a total of 416,797 people vaccinated with their first dose and 232,094 fully vaccinated. With a population of two million in Bexar County, we still had a long way to go.

While vaccinations were the key to stopping the spread of

COVID-19, testing was also still important. Since the beginning of the pandemic the FDA had authorized over 400 COVID-19 test options, including 235 molecular, 88 antibody, and 34 antigen tests.

The FDA had previously approved a PCR test that could be taken at home. You can collect the sample and then mail it to a laboratory for testing. Or you take a rapid antigen test and collect a sample at home, test it using the supplied kit materials, and get results in minutes. Although the rapid antigen test is less reliable than a PCR test, it is still a valuable tool to determine if you are infected. It is more accurate if you have symptoms, achieving 80 percent accuracy compared to a PCR. If the result of the test is negative, it should be confirmed by a PCR test.

In late March 2021 the FDA authorized two rapid at-home COVID-19 antigen tests that could be sold over the counter in drug stores: Abbott Lab's BinaxNOW test and Quidel's Quick-Vue. This was a major step forward, allowing a person easy access to the test at reasonable cost of $14. Within a few months the home tests were flying off the shelves.

***

Schools were struggling with holding classes during the spring semester. NISD Superintendent Brian Woods faced problems getting staff and students to wear face masks and get vaccinations. He had a hard time getting struggling students to return to school and difficulties getting state funding with a declining enrollment.

He told me that 45 percent of elementary students returned, but only 20 percent of middle school children and 6 percent of high school students. As a result, Woods said learning gaps occurred for many students. In many cases remote learning did not stand up to in-person learning. Those students that had less reliable internet connections, less resources, and less support had it far worse than those who had the resources.

STAAR test scores released later in June 2021, showed that one-third of Texas students failed state reading and math assessments. But the results varied among the 16 school districts in San Antonio. While NISD eighth grade test scores were failed by 27 percent of students, those in the minority poor districts, such as Edgewood, failed by 75 percent.

***

As we were enjoying the springtime renewal another crisis emerged that had the potential to impact the spreading of COVID-19 if it was not handled right. We faced a crisis at the Mexico/United States border after President Biden allowed unaccompanied children to cross the border to seek asylum.

He did so because thousands of children who had migrated from Central America through Mexico were living in unsafe conditions on the Mexican side of the border. After he allowed them to cross the border, they were jammed up in temporary camps on the United States side. It was an unsanitary situation that could lead to the spread of COVID-19. I decided to help.

In late March, I began meeting with Bexar County Community Arena's Executive Director Derrick Howard as he began negotiations with the HHS to provide our Exposition Hall as a temporary migrant center. We would provide room for up to 2,100 young boys, age 12–17, who had entered the country and turned themselves in to ask for asylum.

The boys were from the Central American countries of El Salvador, Honduras, and Guatemala. After they had passed through the southern Mexican border they traveled by foot, hitchhiking, or riding buses to the Mexican border towns on the Rio Grande River. On March 25, Howard and I were having lunch at Tony G's when he received a text that said the contract had been signed by HHS. The next day Commissioner Rebeca Clay-Flores, Derrick Howard, and I held a press conference in the Commissioners Court Room where I announced that the county was going to provide a safe haven for the boys for two months in our Exposition Hall. This would give HHS time to locate sponsors and permanent housing until their asylum cases were decided.

As a result of my announcement, I took a couple political punches. Bexar County Sheriff Javier Salazar said, "I do not believe we should agree to house them, and I do not want to allow my deputies to be used." Others stated that the boys would spread COVID-19, but in fact we had large enough facilities to separate those with COVID-19 and properly treat them. Texas Republicans criticized me for supporting immigration of the children and opening the center.

Regardless of who was right or wrong about allowing them to enter the United States, I felt we should provide a safe place for them after they had lived in terrible, overcrowded conditions on the border. I stated that it was a humanitarian effort on the part of Bexar County to offer a safe place.

I joined hundreds of volunteers from Valero and Catholic Charities USA who helped set up 2,100 cots, pillows, and coverings. Two sets of clothing for each boy were organized on tables. RK Catering and Tony G's set up a kitchen and dining hall.

I made several trips to the migrant center as boys arrived by bus. Those who tested positive for COVID-19 were kept in a separate unit for 14 days. CDC officials were on hand to make sure all COVID-19 safety protocols were followed. Homeland Security provided guards to make sure they did not leave the premises.

While everyone was working hard to accommodate the boys, on April 7 Governor Abbott and two Texas Rangers went to the migrant center and held a press conference out front. Abbott stated that he had received complaints about sexual abuse, lack of food, lack of supervision, and improper COVID-19 protocols. He said the center should be shut down.

After making his unfounded assertions, he then took a tour of the facility where Commissioner Rebeca Clay-Flores caught up with him. She said that behind closed doors he was nice to everyone and thanked them. Afterwards Clay Flores stated to the media that he should have done his tour before the press conference, but instead he politicized children.

After gathering all the evidence regarding the governor's allegations, I stated on our daily briefing show that Governor Abbott's claims were false. Time would prove me right as there was no evidence of the governor's assertions and no charges were filed. It was a horrible dehumanizing political stunt by the governor.

On the morning of April 16, I heard that Lieutenant Governor Dan Patrick was on his way to the migrant center. I thought that he might also criticize the center, so I hustled over to meet him. Around noon I walked up to Patrick with my mask on and introduced myself. He responded in a friendly manner, "I know who you are." I thanked him for his support of the revised Alamo plan and said that I wanted to help make the museum happen.

Republican Commissioner Trish DeBerry joined us, and we took a tour of the facility. The Lieutenant Governor talked to the staff of HHS and thanked them for their work. To his credit Patrick never called a media conference or criticized our work at the center.

After visiting the center several times, I paid my last visit on

May 24. Commissioner Clay-Flores joined me to say goodbye to the last two boys who would soon be on their way to Kansas to join their family. We both then spoke to some 200 staff and volunteers.

On May 24, 2021, Judge Wolff and Commissioner Rebeca Clay-Flores thanked all the team that had worked so hard in taking care of the boys at the Bexar County migrant facility.

Clay-Flores thanked them for all their hard work. I praised Derrick Howard and Jose Gonzales, who led the effort for HHS, for their leadership. I thanked Commissioner Clay-Flores for the volunteer work she had done on numerous times at center.

All the false statements by the governor, the opposition of the sheriff, erroneous claims about COVID-19 spreading, and other naysayers were finally put to rest. Bexar County stood up to help children. I was so proud of the humanitarian effort on the part of Bexar County.

***

On May 1, Nirenberg defeated Gregg Brockhouse 61.9 percent to 31.45 percent in the mayoral race. It was a rewarding victory for Nirenberg after Brockhouse came so close to defeating him two years earlier. The fact that Nirenberg provided great leadership throughout the pandemic was recognized by voters. Our daily media briefings gave him a great platform.

A proposition that sought to do away with police collective bargaining barely lost, receiving 48.85 percent of the vote. But it was a clear signal to the union that they needed to seek compromise and back off on attacks against the mayor and council.

One of the disturbing aspects of the non-partisan city election was that people were calling Bexar County Election Administer Jacque Callanen to ask whether a candidate was a Republican or Democrat. Since our non-partisan city elections began, we had kept ugly party politics out of the council and mayoral races. Now it appeared political parties would start endorsing city council candidates.

During the month of May, we concentrated on getting shots into arms at Wonderland Mall. In addition to Wonderland Mall, on May 1 we began offering vaccinations to jail inmates. Within four days we vaccinated 595 inmates.

The city did a great job of opening up testing and vaccination sites in marginalized communities on the south, east, and west sides of town. The COVID-19 Community Response and Equity Coalition and Metro Health led the effort to make sure that everyone had easy access to testing and vaccines.

While we were encouraging people to get vaccinated, we faced a huge pushback from social media postings that have created a culture that makes it difficult to distinguish reality from illusion. Those with political skills manipulate images that overpower reality. Lies, distorted facts, conspiracy theories, fear, and manipulation spread like wildfire. Political dogma became the acid test of what is real and true.

In 2020, the Center for Countering Digital Hate had identified 147 anti-vaccine social media accounts that were putting out false information. They had 51.6 million followers. It was difficult to overcome the voices of the extremists who posted social media warnings such as: COVID-19 vaccines are weapons of mass destruction, they could wipe out the human race, and doctors and nurses who gave the vaccine should be tried as war criminals.

President Biden stated that Facebook platforms were killing people. So Facebook began trying to block the spread of bogus vaccine claims. But Facebook was built on a code written 17 years earlier, and CEO Mark Zuckerberg could not control the machine he created as it spewed out cesspools of anti-vaccination comments. As fast as they eliminated misinformation and lies, other postings rapidly took their place. The disinformation cat had jumped out of the bag and continued scurrying around, leading many people to believe what they heard over social media and refuse to get vaccinated.

A few doctors chimed in with false information such as a physician in Indiana, who stated that vaccines were ineffective and masks did not help stop the spread of COVID-19. He had a large following of millions over social media.

As a result of such postings, the Federation of State Medical Boards recommended that states consider action against doctors who shared false information, including revoking their license. Some states took action against the fallacious doctors.

The people that listened to the false warnings ignored the

fact that many of those not vaccinated were dying. An Associated Press analysis of data from the CDC found in May that 98 percent of the recent 18,000 COVID-19 deaths were those not vaccinated.

Just as disturbing, a poll showed that up to 15 percent of Americans believed in the principles of QAnon, an organization promoting the belief that there is a cabal of liberal elites who worship Satan and traffic children for sex and blood. They allege that there is a "deep state" apparatus run by political elites and business leaders who are pedophiles. As they spread misinformation about COVID-19, President Trump re-tweeted accounts that promoted the QAnon theory more than 200 times.

To counter digital hate and conspiracy messages, some folks turned to an old fashion door-to-door campaign offering yard signs to neighbors. The sign stated: "In this house we believe that science is real, love is love and kindness is everything." If only we had more households that believed in that message.

On May 27, I joined Mayor Nirenberg and several civic leaders organized by my long-time friend Reverend Ann Helmke to reveal a "Deep in our Hearts" memorial to those who had fallen to COVID-19. Along a fence at Hemisfair Park, 3,400 hearts were placed to represent those that had fallen.

By June 1, half of the residents of Bexar County had received one dose of the vaccine and one-third were fully vaccinated, resulting in 885,326 citizens who had been vaccinated with one dose and 558,986 with both doses. On that same day our hospitalized COVID-19 patients had declined to 141 from a high of 1,520 during the winter surge.

Governor Abbott was taking bows declaring that we had contained the spread of COVID-19. People began criticizing Nirenberg and me because we said that the governor had acted too soon when he removed health safeguards three months earlier on March 3.

With COVID-19 apparently under control, on June 3, Mayor Nirenberg and I had our last 4:30 p.m. conference call with health officials and our last media briefing. Our 442nd daily situation report showed we had a total of 224,084 confirmed COVID-19 cases and 3,486 deaths since the pandemic began. But the deaths were likely a lot higher. Serological studies estimate that 35 percent of COVID-19 deaths were unreported.

That night on our last media briefing Mayor Nirenberg emphasized that everyone should get vaccinated. He stated that we needed to expand our efforts to make vaccines easily available. He gave special recognition to Metro Health officials who had guided us through the pandemic including Assistant City Manager Dr. Colleen Bridger, Medical Director Dr. Junda Woo, Assistant Director Jennifer Herriot, Assistant Director Mario Martinez, and Assistant Director Dr. Anita Kurian.

I said over the last 15 months that we had done our best to provide accurate and clear communication, and I thanked everyone for working with us to manage the spread of COVID-19. I also stated that while we have passed the worst, the future is unsure. I said that we also needed to continue researching and preparing for any future pandemic that would surely come our way.

I thanked my Chief of Staff Nicole Erfurth, County Manager David Smith, Public Information Officer Monica Ramos, Commissioners Clay-Flores, DeBerry, Rodriguez, and Calvert, Bexar County Hospital President George Hernandez, Dr. Ruth Berggren, Dr. Bryan Alsip, Seth Mitchell, and our county employees for their hard work and dedication.

On June 6, Mayor Nirenberg, Dr. Colleen Bridger, and Judge Wolff held the last daily media briefing for the next three months. They resumed again when the Delta variant surged.

Local San Antonio television stations including KSAT, KENS, WOAI, KLRN, Telemundo, and Univision gave great coverage of our daily media briefings. They created a huge audience, allowing us to communicate to citizens.

The *San Antonio Express-News* kept up intensive coverage, giving first- and second-page space. Their reporters did a thorough job of writing in-depth articles. There were numerous editorials taking a strong stance supporting professional health experts and the job Nirenberg and I were doing. Publisher Mark Medici, Editor Marc Duvoisin, and editorial writer Josh Brodesky led an effort to provide accurate information to thousands of readers.

Former *Express-News* editor Bob Rivard started an all-digital newspaper format, now called *San Antonio Report*. Through the COVID-19 crisis he kept a team of reporters covering the issues, and he also personally wrote several COVID-19 editorials.

While I was relieved to end the daily media briefings and conference calls, at the same time I felt a void, missing my daily communication with my colleagues as we worked our way through the pandemic. I had grown close to them as we plotted our course. I also missed being with Nirenberg as we communicated with our citizens, doing our best to keep them safe with our emergency orders and advice. But as we would soon see, the end was not here, and we would have to reengage.

With the passage of the American Rescue Plan, I was amazed that Bexar County would be allocated $388 million and the city $326 million. It was like finding a rich uncle who had died and left me a huge fortune. In this case it was Uncle Joe, the newly elected president.

During the pandemic County Manager David Smith watched every penny that was spent to keep our budget balanced with our falling revenue. Now suddenly, we had this financial windfall giving us an opportunity to invest in what I hoped would be sustainable development projects that would create jobs and provide services to our citizens.

Under the 2020 CARES Act Fund we had to spend the money in nine months because Congress wanted money out the window quickly to help businesses and citizens who were in a financial crisis. Under the leadership of Executive Director of Community Development David Marquez, we allocated $19,836,000 in $25,000 grants to 1,200 small business, $8.7 million to suburban cities, $5.5 million to arts and culture, $6.3 million to mental health programs, $6.3 million to education, $7.2 million to housing assistance and social services, and $3.1 million to workforce.

In addition to the CARES Act funding for job training, we budgeted $10 million to build at an advanced manufacturing center at Brooks City Base. Bexar County Economic Director David Marquez developed a partnership with the Texas Federation for Advanced Manufacturing to provide the training.

Under the American Rescue Plan, we had three years to make financial commitments and five years to spend the money. The Commissioners Court instructed the county manager to enter a contract with Guidehouse, a consulting firm, to help us navigate the financial rules that would be written by the Treasury Department. Smith set up an office headed by his Chief of Staff Thomas Guevara to oversee the distribution of funds.

One of the first economic development projects we funded was a grant to the Alamo Museum. The restoration of the Alamo and the museum would have a major impact on our tourism industry that had been devastated.

Commissioner DeBerry and I co-authored the county funding grant in the amount of $25 million paid out at $5 million per year for the next five years. We were getting 10 times leverage for the money we were putting up. We pointed out that a study found that the project would have an economic impact on San Antonio in the amount of $430 million and create 3,495 new jobs.

At our May 18 Commissioner Court meeting, Lieutenant Governor Patrick and Land Commissioner George P. Bush addressed the court on Zoom. Patrick spoke from his office that was chockfull of Alamo artifacts. He stated his commitment to the Alamo and his promise to seek more state funding. Land Commissioner Bush spoke of his support for the new plan and thanked us for the contribution.

The court then approved the financial commitment on a 5–0 vote. Later the state legislature used Bexar County's commitment to leverage another $175 million from the state. We also approved $4 million for a housing project for people 50 and older who had mental and physical health problems. We also approved $4 million for Lifetime Recovery advocated by Commissioner Clay-Flores to build and staff 60 additional beds for the treatment of alcohol and drugs.

By the end of spring, on June 19, it appeared the governor was right. We were down to 122 COVID-19 hospitalizations and our positivity rate was only 1.3 percent. So, Nirenberg and I looked like alarmists when we did not agree with the governor opening up Texas on March 3.

But we would soon find out Mr. COVID had developed a new powerful self that spread much faster, and he was coming to see us. It had been detected in December 2020 when it began spreading in India. Later it jumped to Great Britain and continental Europe. And now for the second time Governor Abbott would be caught asleep at the wheel as Mr. COVID sailed and flew across the blue Atlantic Ocean to the sunny shores of America.

8. Surprise Attack of The Delta Force

AS WE NEARED THE END of June the Delta force came ashore. Some 25 states, after a steady decline, were reporting higher seven-day averages of infections. As it quickly spread, health experts believed that the Delta variant was about twice as contagious as the original COVID-19 strain. Some research suggested that Delta carried a load a thousand times more viral than the original COVID-19 and that people may stay infected longer. COVID-19 had indeed armed up.

In May, the CDC had stopped tracking breakthrough infections of vaccinated people unless they were hospitalized (very few were at this time). That left the question of whether an asymptomatic vaccinated person could be infected and spread the virus. As a result of the lack of information the CDC had recommended that only the unvaccinated should wear a mask.

Some experts predicted a major surge in the southern states because of low vaccination rates. Texas was a candidate because the state had ranked low in vaccinations with only 61 percent receiving at least one shot. It did not help that Governor Abbott signed legislation that penalized businesses that required customers to show proof of vaccination.

Although Texas lagged behind other large states in vaccinations, our close neighbors had worse vaccination rates. The states of Mississippi, Louisiana, and Alabama had about half the vaccination rate of northern states. And our neighbors were on the move, some coming to our city as our tourism industry was making a comeback. With the threatening Delta variant, we pushed to increase our vaccination rate. We were happy to greet Homeland Security Secretary Alejandro Mayorkas who had come to Texas to promote vaccinations. On June 30 Mayor Nirenberg and I met him at our mass UHS vaccination center at Wonderland.

Along with UHS President George Hernandez, Vice President Bill Phillips, and Commissioner Justin Rodriguez, we took a tour of the site. Phillips, who ran the mass vaccination site, explained the operation to Mayorkas.

I told Mayorkas that I had been by several different times to meet with staff and visit with people who had their shots while they were waiting the required 15 minutes to be observed. I said the hospital staff treated the patients with kindness and everyone had praise for them.

At a follow-up press conference, Mayor Nirenberg announced that San Antonio had exceeded President Joe Biden's vaccination goal. We had provided one dose to 72.6 percent of our citizens and two doses to 57.7 percent. That resulted in 1,207,058 people who had at least one dose and 959,040 who had both doses.

I stated that our mass vaccination site at Wonderland had reached a high, giving over 7,500 vaccinations in one day. Secretary Mayorkas said, "What San Antonio will be able to deliver is normalcy more quickly to its residents and I hope that other cities see what San Antonio has done as a result of their vaccination effort."

June 21. Mayor Nirenberg, Homeland Security Secretary Alejandro Mayorkas, Judge Wolff, UHS Vice President Bill Phillips, and UHS President George Hernandez confer at UHS Wonderland mass vaccination site.

Actually, the numbers we reported were for the two million citizens of Bexar County. More than 2,000 counties, representing approximately half of the United States' population, had not met President Biden's goal. Bexar County was one of the rare urban counties to succeed.

Other vaccination sites complimented UHS and the city's mass vaccination at the Alamodome. CentroMed President Ernesto Gomez set up vaccination sites at their 20 clinics located throughout Bexar County. UT Health and WellMed clinics offered shots. In July pharmacies and grocery stores also began offering shots.

The UHS Wonderland mass vaccination site was by far the largest local provider of vaccine shots. At this point, UHS had administered 413,042 shots at Wonderland, as well as 11,119 shots at the hospital, 30,970 at the Robert B. Green clinic, 1,545 in the clinics and pharmacy, and 20,027 in a partnership with colleges and churches.

We could not have been successful without the tremendous work of the pharmacy industry. Over the last six months the industry distributed 320 million doses. While doing so, the federal government richly compensated them. For example, Moderna received $955 million for the development of the vaccine and was paid $1.525 billion for 100 million doses. Their total sales for the year were approximately $20 billion.

As July days flew by, we were headed toward a Delta surge caused in large part by the unvaccinated. On July 14 we had 258 COVID-19 patients in the hospital, with the unvaccinated accounting for over 88 percent of the COVID-19 patients. On that same day the Texas Department of Health and Human Services reported that 99.5 percent of 8,787 COVID-19 deaths since February 8 were unvaccinated.

Even as the unvaccinated faced hospitalization and possible death, their roar reached a new height in July at the Conservative Political Action Conference where speakers were cheered when they made anti-vaccination assertions. Dr. Anthony Fauci said it was frightening and horrifying to listen to them. "How can people cheer for death?" he asked.

At a media conference that day, I pointed out that only about 30 percent of people ages 15–29 had been fully vaccinated. I warned them that they could face long-term debilitating consequences from COVID-19 such as severe fatigue, cognitive issues, memory lapses, digestive problems, and a host of other complications if they did not get vaccinated.

Mayor Nirenberg stated that COVID-19 was not finished with us. He encouraged people to get vaccinations and enumerated all the various places they could get vaccinated. He thanked volunteers for going house-to-house to encourage people to get vaccinated.

But our warning did not do much good among the hardcore who refused to get vaccinated. It is a trite saying but as they say, you can lead a horse to water, but you can't make him drink. A July 23 poll by the Associated Press-NORC Center for Public Affairs Research showed that of the 35 percent of American adults who had not been vaccinated, 45 percent of them said they definitely would not get the vaccine.

A few days later *The New York Times* did a survey of people who chose not to get vaccinated. Those who were adamant in their refusal tended to be disproportionately white, rural, evangelical Christians, and politically conservative. But also young, lower income, and less educated people were in the adamant group. Sixty-seven percent of the adamant were Republicans as opposed to 12 percent that were Democrats. The unvaccinated had various reasons for refusing shots.

Among them were concerns about side effects and the distrust of vaccines and government; people refused the vaccine because they didn't believe they needed it, they didn't like vaccines, and they wanted final FDA approval. While 45 percent of the unvaccinated made it clear they would never get the vaccination, we had a chance to reach the 55 percent who said they might be persuaded. They were mostly younger people, Black, Latino, and Democrats.

On July 23 Nirenberg and I met with the CEOs of our four largest hospital systems at our joint emergency center. With 415 COVID-19 patients in the hospital they were concerned about a staffing shortage because many nurses had quit or took early retirement because of fatigue. If things got worse, they agreed to consider canceling elective surgeries.

We followed up with a letter to Governor Abbott on July 28 citing the need for the Texas Division of Emergency Management (TDEM) to send us nurses as they did during the previous two COVID-19 waves. We also urged the governor to reinstate our authority to mandate masks.

We did get a response from the governor, but one we did not like. He refused to allow us to mandate masks. And then he had W. Nim Kidd, Chief of TDEM, send out a notice that they would not contract for nurses and that we should pay for them locally.

The state had been reimbursed $5.9 billion from FEMA for previous nurses and respiratory therapists during the last two COVID-19 waves; 1,600 nurses and respiratory therapists were provided for our hospitals. I told the media that there had been so many failures by the state that it was hard to enumerate all of them, but this one was totally unnecessary because the cost was fully refundable by FEMA.

I then talked with Tony Robinson, FEMA regional director, who stated that they would continue to reimburse if the state submitted a request. After I talked with W. Nim Kidd, he agreed to forward any request for reimbursement to FEMA if we paid for the nurses. We were prepared to do so if our patient load increased.

Many nurses in Texas had accepted contracts from other states where they could make as much as $1,600 a week. As Texas continued to lose nurses, finally Governor Abbott woke up two weeks later and reversed his previous decision and allowed TDEM to contract for nurses. We were glad to see the reversal, but it was coming late in the game. It would take at least a week to round up the nurses. We finally did initially secure 295 nurses.

I also talked with Army North Commander Lieutenant General Laura J. Richardson, whose command is located at Ft. Sam

Houston in San Antonio. She was in Washington when I asked her if Army North would again be providing nurses. She said she would seek approval to do so.

In August Richardson announced that Army North would again draw medical teams from the Navy, Air Force, and Army to help defeat COVID-19. By the way, Richardson was promoted to a four-star general, and she would soon take command of the U.S. Southern Command, one of eleven Pentagon combatant commands.

On July 27, the CDC recommended that the vaccinated should also wear face masks. After an outbreak in Provincetown, Massachusetts, they found that the Delta variant had infected some of the vaccinated, including those who were asymptomatic, and that they could then infect others.

Unfortunately, the CDC recommendation was behind the curve. They should have paid attention to what happened in May in Great Britain when their centralized health care system quickly gathered data on how and when people got infected. From the collected data they determined that the Delta variant was infecting two-thirds more than the original COVID-19 and vaccinated people were susceptible to the Delta variant even though serious symptoms would be rare.

Had the CDC acted earlier, we could have slowed down the spread of the super contagious Delta. To be fair to them, they were hampered by our private and decentralized health care system, making it harder to quickly collect data. Great Britain had the advantage of a centralized health care system that could quickly collect data.

In June, data released from Singapore further demonstrated that the vaccinated could get the Delta variant and spread it. High quality contact tracing provided the data they needed.

Four days after the new CDC recommendation to mask the vaccinated, another systematic study from Singapore showed that the Delta variant quickly peaked and then crashed in breakthrough cases of vaccinated people. The infectious period is much longer in the unvaccinated who have an average of 8.9 days compared to 2.7 days for vaccinated.

A later CDC study showed that only one in 5,000 cases of the Delta variant were found in vaccinated people. It was even lower if a person took precautions and lived in a high vaccination community—as low as one in 10,000 cases.

The CDC also found that the unvaccinated were 10 times more likely to be hospitalized and 11 times more likely to die from COVID-19. We would find that to be true in our community.

On that same day of the CDC recommendation, Nirenberg and I had a WebEx conference with health officials and school superintendents. We explained the difficult task they may face if the Delta variant continued to spread after the school year began. We asked them to put pressure on the governor to allow them to impose mandatory face masks if the Delta variant continued to spread.

It was important to protect children in school because COVID-19, as well as respiratory syncytial virus (RSV), was spreading. RSV is a common virus that is very contagious and infects the respiratory tract of children. As we headed into the fall without a mask mandate in schools, it looked like children would be facing a triple threat of flu, COVID-19, and RSV.

By the first of August, 98.6 percent of the positive cases in Bexar County were the Delta variant. That was a sharp rise from 16 percent in May. We were now facing a much more dangerous variant that grows efficiently in the upper respiratory tract.

The unvaccinated and the unmasked were allowing the Delta variant to continue to spread. The longer it continued to spread, the more it could mutate into an even more dangerous variant that could even render existing vaccines useless.

On August 5, Texas surpassed New York in COVID-19 deaths for a total of 53,275 deaths. It was a reversal from last summer when Texas had 29,000 fewer deaths than New York. Since last summer, twice as many Texans as New Yorkers have died from COVID-19, clearly showing the results of the governor taking away mandatory health safety measures. As a result, President Biden blasted governors who were standing in the way of health safety measures, noting that Texas and Florida accounted for two-thirds of all new COVID-19 cases.

I called Nirenberg on Sunday morning, August 8, as I sat outside in my courtyard reading *The New York Times*. I suggested that we hold a media conference the next day at the monoclonal infusion center that we were reopening after it had closed in March when everyone thought COVID-19 was under control.

He agreed and then said he had directed City Attorney Andy Segovia to prepare a lawsuit against the governor asserting that he had violated state statues and the constitution by restricting our local authority. We had talked numerous times about suing the governor for exceeding his authority, so I was happy to hear that Segovia was working on a lawsuit. Nirenberg stated that we needed to go after the root of the problem—Abbott's abuse of power. We agreed to meet with our legal teams the next day.

District Attorney Joe Gonzales, Assistant District Attorney Larry Roberson, Commissioner Justin Rodriguez, and I walked over to City Hall from the courthouse at 1:00 p.m. on Monday to meet Nirenberg and his legal team. After Segovia laid out the proposed city lawsuit, I said I was not happy with it and that I thought it should be a joint lawsuit with the county. I also stated that Nirenberg and I should be leading the lawsuit.

The city lawyers began to realize they were coming to our house to file the lawsuit and if they wanted a better chance to win, they would need us. They agreed to continue to meet with Assistant District Attorney Roberson to work it out. Roberson later drew up a new version of a joint lawsuit, and it was accepted with a small modification by the city.

While the lawyers worked on the lawsuit, Nirenberg and I went to the infusion center located at the Bexar County Exposition Center. At the press conference held there we announced that the infusion center would open the following morning at 8:00 a.m. and had the capacity to do 150 infusions of REGEN-COV each day for free.

At 8:00 p.m. that night Nirenberg and I had a conference call with our legal teams and agreed to file the lawsuit at 9:00 a.m. the following morning. The lawsuit asked for a restraining order against the governor, allowing the public health authority, Dr. Junda Woo, to mandate face masks in schools, and for the right of Nirenberg and I to require face masks in all county and city facilities.

At 7:00 a.m. the next morning, August 10, I signed an order directing the district attorney to file the lawsuit on behalf of the county. I also signed an affidavit stating the danger of the Delta variant.

While the suit was being filed Tuesday morning, I convened the Commissioners Court's meeting. UHS President George Hernandez testified that the average age of Delta COVID-19 hospital patients dropped from 61 to 54 and that 92.7 percent were not vaccinated. When he presented a chart showing a vertical rise in COVID-19 hospital cases to 1,197, I stopped him and announced the filing of the lawsuit and that the case was set for a hearing that afternoon at 1:30 p.m.

On August 8, District Attorney Joe Gonzales, Judge Wolff, and Mayor Nirenberg held a press conference announcing that the District Court had granted a temporary restraining order against Governor Abbott's emergency order that sought to prevent mandatory face masks for school children.

We continued the court meeting and passed an incentive plan for our employees to get vaccinated. We offered a refund of their share of premium payments for health insurance for 2021 with a cap of $1,000 if they showed evidence of being vaccinated by October 15.

Employees who refused to be vaccinated citing their religious beliefs would not be eligible for the bonus. We were backed up by San Antonio Archbishop Gustavo Garcia-Siller who said the archdiocese will not provide religious exemption letters to people who objected to receive a COVID-19 vaccination. He stated he does not consider the COVID-19 vaccine to be morally objectionable.

In addition to the vaccine bonus, we approved $319,517 for a vaccine advertising campaign that included 33 billboard locations around the county, specifically in low income and underserved areas on the east, west, and south side. These funds supplemented the city's funding for advertising. The city also began implementation of a plan to provide a $100 gift card to anyone willing to get vaccinated.

The Commissioners Court also approved funding for a $15 million incentive package to a partnership between the Spurs organization and USAA to build a $510.8 million human performance center that would focus on creativity, physical, mindfulness, technology, nutrition, medical, and life skills.

The human performance center project was important because many of our COVID-19-related deaths were because of underlying health conditions. A later study by *The Wall Street Journal* found that older people and those with underlying health issues such as diabetes, chronic lung disease, kidney disease, and compromised immune systems were at risk of serious outcomes in breakthrough cases of the vaccinated.

The project also included a 22-acre park with a walking path and amenities as well as an area for dogs, paid for by USAA. The park would be deeded to Bexar County, giving us a safe green environment for people. It also included a new entrance to the nature trails along the Leon Creek. A few weeks later the San Antonio

City Council committed $17 million to the project.

Later that day at 3:30 p.m. Roberson called and said we had received a temporary restraining order against the governor issued by Judge Toni Arteaga. A hearing on the permanent injunction would be held the following Monday. At 4:00 p.m. Nirenberg, DA Joe Gonzales, and I held a media conference in front of City Hall announcing the victory.

That night we held our first media briefing after a lull of three months. We agreed to have them every Tuesday and Thursday. At the first media briefing we stated it was up to the schools to enforce a mask mandate. Without their support the order would have no effect.

There are 16 school districts in Bexar County, and I suspected that compliance would be spotty. Some would be concerned that the Texas Supreme Court would quickly overrule Judge Arteaga's order.

Jane McCurley, chief nursing executive at Methodist Hospital, joined our briefing and announced she had never seen such a display of ugliness by some COVID-19 patients and their families, even to the extent of threatening nurses. Some of the unvaccinated were taking their frustration of their self-imposed sickness out on health care workers. Methodist Hospital had to increase security.

It was heartbreaking to hear McCurley's story about nurse abuse at a time when they were putting their lives at risk everyday treating COVID-19 patients. Many health care workers had died trying to save COVID-19 patients.

On September 7, 2021, the CDC reported that 1,740 health care workers had died in the United States treating COVID-19 patients since the pandemic began. The National Nurses United previously stated that a little over 1,700 deaths had occurred among health care workers in the year 2020 alone. According to *The Guardian* United States edition, 3,607 health care workers died since the pandemic began.

The count was uncertain because the Trump administration had taken the responsibility away from the CDC and had given it to the HHS, who in turn relied on state reporting and the states to provide accurate counts. Today no one has an accurate count.

While we have focused our attention on frontline doctors and nurses who care for the patients, there is also a large contingent of health care workers who do the hard work of making physical conditions safe. They sanitize emergency rooms, make beds, dispose of used needles and other paraphernalia, and clean blood off the floor, putting their lives at risk—for less pay.

Not only were the unvaccinated endangering health care workers, they also were endangering the lives of senior citizens in nursing homes. Active cases of the Delta variant in nursing homes across the nation had tripled within the month of August. According to the Centers for Medicaid & Medicare services, 15 states only had 48 percent of nursing home staffers that were fully vaccinated. Massachusetts had to mandate vaccines for nursing home staff after finding 41 percent of 378 nursing homes had vaccination rates below average.

The unruly unvaccinated patients and families at the Methodist Hospital were joined by defiant anti-mask travelers. The Federal Aviation Administration assessed fines totaling more than $1 million against 3,889 recalcitrant passengers. Some had thrown things at people, tried to break into cockpits, and assaulted crew members. Of the 3,889 violations, 2,876 were related to face masks. That night I issued my 21st emergency order requiring face masks for employees and visitors in all county facilities. I also required businesses to post their safety requirements, including face mask mandates, if they chose to do so. I stated that if they chose to mandate face masks and someone resisted, law enforcement would respond to their call. City Manager Erik Walsh set a face mask requirement for employees and anyone visiting city facilities.

The following day, Attorney General Ken Paxton announced he would appeal directly to the Supreme Court to strike down all local face mask requirements, including school mandates. Governor Abbott chimed in threatening to sue schools if they put in place a mask mandate.

Governor Abbott and Attorney General Paxton were putting children at risk at time when the CDC reported that increased child hospitalization rates were driven by states such as Texas and Florida. Both states had banned mandated health safety measures for schools. As a result, Texas' COVID-19 child hospitalization rate for the first week of August was the highest in over one year.

The CDC also reported that in the last week pediatric cases rose by 94,000 in the nation, a 31 percent increase over the last week. The American Academy of Pediatrics also released a statement on August 5, stating that 4.1 million children had contacted COVID-19 since the pandemic began, 14.3 percent of all cases. At our media briefing I cited the above information and said that is why we were fighting in court to overturn Abbott's order that prevented us from protecting children.

Nirenberg revealed that EMS had reached its high point in COVID-19 related transportation to the hospital with 117 calls. With 39 EMS units, they were stretched beyond capacity, and for 26 minutes they were unable to respond to demand.

At 5:00 p.m. on Saturday afternoon the city and county legal team filed a 35-page response with the Texas Supreme Court stating the merits of our case. After reading our response I was convinced we were right ethically and legally. We alleged that Abbott's only authority should be to suspend local orders that would in any way prevent, hinder, or delay necessary action in coping with a disaster. Clearly, we were not doing that.

But sad to say the following day Sunday, August 15, the Texas Supreme Court ruled that the temporary restraining order issued by Judge Arteaga was suspended. But they did not dismiss our lawsuit, so we were back in Judge Arteaga's court on Monday for a hearing on a temporary injunction against the governor's order.

During the seven-hour hearing held over Zoom, County Manager David Smith, City Manager Eric Walsh, and Dr. Junda Woo testified. They presented a strong case for the danger of the Delta variant and legal arguments establishing that Governor Abbott had exceeded his authority.

The attorney general presented only one witness, a mother who did not want her child to be forced to wear a face mask. I assumed he was confident that they would eventually prevail in the Texas Supreme Court.

Judge Arteaga granted a temporary injunction against the governor's emergency order until a trial date that was set for December 13. The attorney general appealed to the Fourth Court of Appeals.

On the following day, August 16, Governor Abbott announced that he had tested positive for COVID-19. He had been to a Republican rally in Collin County the day before where he did not wear a face mask and neither did most of the other Republicans at the rally. He did not have any symptoms, but to be safe he was administered a monoclonal antibody treatment to hopefully prevent him from getting sick. He also had been vaccinated and escaped unharmed.

A nationwide poll by the Axious-Ipsos Coronavirus Index was released on August 17 that revealed that two-thirds of Americans were opposed to the prohibition of face coverings such as Governor Abbott ordered. But unfortunately, 57 percent of Republicans supported the state banning mandatory face masks. That is why Governor Abbott changed his position from supporting face mask mandates to opposing them. He was facing two Republican Attila-the-Hun-like challengers who had criticized him for previously mandating face masks.

On August 18 at our Thursday media briefing, I stated that SAISD Superintendent Pedro Martinez deserved a badge of honor because he was sued by the attorney general for requiring SAISD employees to be vaccinated. Nirenberg announced that the Fourth Court of Appeals had upheld Arteaga's temporary injunction against the governor.

On August 19, TEA issued a public health guidance to all public schools. As part of the guidance, they stated that the mask prohibition provisions of the governor's emergency order would not be enforced because of the ongoing litigation.

That is why our lawsuit was so important, for without it, the governor's anti mask order would have been enforced. This was a significant guidance as it allowed school districts to mandate masks if they chose to. It was now up to the school boards to protect their children or let the Delta variant spread unchecked.

President Biden jumped in to help and directed the U.S. Department of Education to take action against governors that prevented schools from mandating face masks. I was not sure they had any authority to do so.

A new Texas poll by Spectrum News/Ipsos on August 19 showed 72 percent support for school face mask mandates.

We received good news on August 23, when the FDA granted full approval to the Pfizer-BioNTech coronavirus vaccine for people 16 and older. This removed one of the reasons why people had stated they did not want to be vaccinated.

On that same day U.S. Secretary of Defense Lloyd Austin announced that the 1.4 million active-duty service members will have to be vaccinated. The military has a long history of protecting their troops from viruses.

During our war for independence smallpox killed about one-third of our soldiers who had been infected and left many others scarred for life. It had doomed the American assault on Quebec in 1775 and now threatened General George Washington's main force. Washington embraced science-based medical treatments and required his troops to be vaccinated against smallpox, going against the direction of the Continental Congress.

By the end of 1777 around 40,000 soldiers had been vaccinated. As a result of his order, infection rates dropped from 20 percent to 1 percent. Without his decisive action requiring vaccinations, we may not have won our war for independence.

On August 23 the FDA posted a warning on Twitter, "You are not a horse. You are not a cow. Seriously, y'all. Stop it." The Mississippi State Department of Health had stated in an alert that at least two people had been hospitalized with ivermectin toxicity after ingesting the drug that is produced for livestock. The drug is toxic to humans and can cause hallucinations, tremors, and confusion.

Even though the FDA warned Americans not to take ivermectin, people continued to ingest it. The Poison Control network reported 260 calls about ivermectin poisoning. The use was driven by false assurances, such as by a Fox News host who said that you could use the drug to treat COVID-19. Social media yapping hounds spread the word. Locally the demand was so crazy that Johnny's Feed and Supply took ivermectin off the shelf and refused to sell because so many customers were taking it to treat COVID-19.

A study in the CDC's Morbidity and Mortality Weekly Report released on the same day showed that unvaccinated people were 29 times more likely to be hospitalized than the vaccinated. They also were nearly five times more likely to be infected than the vaccinated.

On Thursday, August 26, the Texas Supreme Court overruled the Fourth Court of Appeals' temporary injunction, but again they did not set aside our lawsuit. So, schools could still mandate masks because TEA had stated that they would not enforce Abbott's emergency order as long as our litigation was pending.

But local district attorneys could take action against school districts' mandated mask policy. I received a text message from NISD Superintendent Brian Woods who asked me to talk with District Attorney Joe Gonzales to assure the school districts that he would not prosecute them for violating Abbott's order.

I talked with Gonzales, and he agreed to not prosecute school officials as long as TEA continued their guidance. He made his statement public, and I sent it to Woods. So the NISD board voted to mandate masks.

By now most of our local public school districts, including NISD, SAISD, Northeast Independent School District (NEISD), and Alamo Heights independent School District, had passed a mandatory face mask policy. In our media briefing on August 26, we stated that our local school districts were doing the right thing by mandating face coverings, and we supported them 100 percent. Flu, RSV, and COVID-19 can be largely prevented by face coverings. I went on to say it is so distressing that the governor and the attorney general are doing everything he can to stop us from protecting children.

Meanwhile the number of COVID-19 hospitalized adult patients began to stabilize. On our September 2 media briefing I attributed the slowdown of hospitalized patients in part to the fact that we had younger COVID-19 patients who could recover more quickly and our enhanced medical procedures.

At the same time, we were having success at the infusion center where 2,249 COVID-19 patients had been infused with monoclonal antibodies since we opened a few weeks earlier. In the last seven days we were averaging 120 fusion patients a day.

The Centers for Medicare and Medicaid Services approved UHS's plan for "hospital at home." Conditions at home must be safe and be within 20 miles of a hospital. The patient must have access to a dedicated nurse line 24 hours a day. UHS began the program on July 17, opening up 45 days of available hospital beds.

***

On Sunday, September 5 around 1:00 p.m., when I was coming out of the Alon H-E-B grocery store, a woman followed me out to my car. As I walked along pushing my grocery cart, she began spewing a fusillade of words of hate and anger at me as she recorded the event with her phone.

In about a three-minute rising verbal cascade she called me a communist, a traitor, and a horrible person; she screamed, asking me how I am supporting the devil and not God. She said, enjoy your freedom while it lasts, you're going down, you won't be able to walk the streets for long, and they are going to hang you. She described the COVID-19 vaccine as a bioweapon. When she said the election was rigged, I knew she was one of Trump's supporters. I kept my cool, ignored her, loaded my groceries, and drove off.

When I arrived home, I spoke about the incident with my

wife Tracy. After relating the encounter, I said that it's interesting that I feel no anger or fear, but instead a deep sorrow about the ingrained hate, anger, conspiracy theories, and false information that occurs over social media and is now embedded in so many people.

Tracy had a different take and felt that people like her should be held accountable because she could have an impact on others who could resort to violence. That certainly was a possibility. Word got out about the encounter on the same day. I declined media calls.

The next day the charming lady released the video of the encounter on her social media site and stated to the *San Antonio Express-News* that she wanted to encourage others to follow her example. I was grateful that she released it because the video spoke for itself, and I did not have to describe the encounter to the media. That night on our media briefing show I said, "People pick up those terrible views over the internet and then they espouse the same views." I said I would not be intimidated by things people said and would live a normal life. I continued to urge people to mask-up, keep a social distance, and keep up sanitary practices. Nirenberg said, "That is as big of a disease right now in our community and nation as anything else."

In a follow up article in the *San Antonio Express-News* St. Mary's University law professor Donna Coltharp, who specializes in criminal law, stated as despicable as she thought the woman's behavior was, she was in the legal limits of the law because she implied others would do the dirty deed. While I agreed with the good professor, I wondered whether the parking lot lady had inspired others to take violent action after I learned some 21,000 people looked at the video and several agreed with her. I decided to stay out of dark alleys.

***

While Governor Abbott had taken a nose dive in Bexar County polls, he was now dropping hard throughout the state. In a Texas Politics Project poll of 1,200 registered Texas voters, only 41 percent approved of his job performance and 50 percent disapproved. When asked about the COVID-19 crisis, only 39 percent approved and 53 percent disapproved. His political posturing had not helped him by changing his views from the early stage of COVID-19 when he exhibited great leadership.

On our Thursday, September 9 media briefing we announced that COVID-19-related deaths had reach a new milestone, exceeding 4,000 deaths—rising by 400 in the last six weeks. I stated that many of the deaths were completely unnecessary because people had refused to get vaccinated.

On the same day President Biden shocked everyone when he announced that a coming rule of the federal Occupational Safety and Health Administration would require any company with over 100 employees to have their workers vaccinated or take a weekly COVID-19 test. Workers at health facilities that receive federal Medicare and Medicaid would also have to be vaccinated. He had already mandated vaccination for all federal workers. He also doubled the fine for people violating mask mandates on planes, trains, and other public transportation.

Not to be outdone by the president, Texas Attorney General Paxton struck back along with attorney generals from 24 other states to file lawsuits in federal court to stop the president's mandate.

Later Governor Abbott issued an emergency order on October 10 that banned any entity in Texas, including private businesses, from requiring vaccinations for employees or customers. Previously an Abbott spokesman had said in August that private businesses didn't need government running their business.

Actually, companies were giving employees a choice of a weekly COVID-19 test or vaccination. I remembered when Nirenberg and I were forced to take a COVID-19 test before we met with the governor at the airport on August 4, 2020. A bit of hypocrisy!

Paxton also sued nine school districts over masking requirements even though he originally said he would leave it up to local district attorneys and even though TEA was not enforcing Abbott's ban on face masks. One school superintendent described his action as a "cowardly move."

We had turned the corner and were headed toward managing the Delta variant by September 14. On our media briefing, Nirenberg announced that our positivity rate was down to 7.1 percent and hospitalization down to 1,016 from a high of 1,466. Still, it was no time to declare victory, but optimism was in the air.

On the same day the Commissioners Court adopted a $2.79 billion budget that included a small tax cut, a 5 percent raise for employees, and an increase of 32 new positions in the four constable offices and 17 in the sheriff's office for a total of 49 new law enforcement positions.

Included in the budget was a 10-year $617 million infrastructure plan developed under the leadership of Renee Green, Director of Public Works. We budgeted $167.7 million for roads, $110.7 million for flood control, $74.4 million for parks, and $244.2 million for creeks and trails.

From the summer 2020 COVID-19 surge, to the winter 2021 surge, and now to the Delta surge, our nation had become polarized along political lines and seen the rise of the conspiracy hate club. The trauma of COVID-19 led to an attempted recall of California Governor Gavin Newsom, a Democrat, over his strong action to control the spread of the virus. The campaign turned into a national campaign when it was cast as a Trump-inspired recall effort—which it was. The anti-Newsom campaign was led by a right-wing radio show host. Newsom prevailed by a large margin of 64 percent to 36 percent on September 15. That was good news whether you were a Republican or Democrat and believed in protecting people from COVID-19.

COVID-19 deaths nationally now exceeded the 675,000 deaths from the flu epidemic in 1918. One in every 500 Americans had succumbed to the virus. With COVID-19 deaths reaching nearly 2,000 a day, it was not over for the unvaccinated who made up over 90 percent of the deaths.

By the middle of September, we had administered over 5,000 infusions at the Bexar County Expo Hall at a cost of approximately $2,100 to taxpayers for each infusion (compared to the vaccination cost of only $20). Because of the demand for infusions from the unvaccinated, health officials announced that demand for monoclonal antibodies administered by infusion would outstrip supply. The seven low vaccination states in the south were taking 70 percent of the supply. Texas and Florida were getting the most doses, 26,640 and 30,950.

While supplies for infusions were threatened, research continued into the development of a pill that could be used in place of the monoclonal antibody therapies that we were administering at the Bexar County Expo Hall. The pill developed by Merck and Ridgeback Biotherapeutics showed promising results in trials. Early trials were successful and could cut hospitalizations and deaths in half for those with mild to moderate COVID-19. It would be similar to Tamiflu that shortens the illness by one day and blunts severe symptoms.

The pill, known as molnupiravir, would have to be prescribed by a doctor. It is recommended that a person takes 40 pills over five days within 24 hours of showing symptoms and getting tested. Although it was less effective than the monoclonal infusions, it was expected to be less expensive, about one-third of the cost. Merck asked the FDA for approval.

Pfizer developed a pill known as Paxlovid. Trials have shown that is even more effective than molunpiravir. If taken within three days of diagnosis it is 89 percent effective in preventing hospitalization for those with mild to moderate COVID-19. Patients must take 30 pills over five days and another antiviral pill called ritonavir.

A study by the CDC found that 93 percent of Moderna and 88 percent of Pfizer-BioNTech vaccines protected people from being hospitalized but that they would lose their effectiveness as time passes. A study conducted by Kaiser Permanente found that the Pfizer vaccine loses its effectiveness from its high of 88 percent to as low as 47 percent. The vaccinated who were hospitalized were those with the longest timeline from their first vaccinations. But even with the downtick, up to 90 percent of those vaccinated prevented hospitalization. That is why the booster shot is important.

According to an article by Yale Medicine, the Johnson & Johnson (J&J) one shot vaccine only had an effectiveness of 71 percent. Unlike the Pfizer-BioNTech and Moderna vaccines, J&J does not use the mRNA vaccine. Instead, it uses an adenovirus vector as the basis for their vaccine. It is still effective but appears to be not as effective as the other two.

On Friday, September 24, we reopened our mass vaccination site at Wonderland to offer the FDA-approved Pfizer vaccine booster shot for those over 65 years old and people who had serious underlying health issue. I took my sister-in-law Johnny Mae Davideck, and we both got our shots in the back room where the vaccines were being prepared. I visited with all the staff and thanked them for their work. Tracy had received her booster the day before at UT Health. One thousand nine hundred were vaccinated on the first day. I was happy to see the large turnout.

On September 17 TEA reversed their previous policy and stated that schools could not require masks for students and staff. They caved into Governor Abbott's political pressure ban. Sadly, it was coming at a time when, according to the Texas Department of State Health Services, over 154,444 Texas school children had been infected with COVID-19. The number of cases is clearly an under-count because school districts are required to report COVID-19 cases, and many did not adequately report their numbers. Also, by the second week of September the number of children locally hospi-talized hit an all-time high of 345 on September 4.

School districts that stood up and required face masks from the start of the school year were successful in holding down the number of COVID-19 cases. The CDC did an analysis of 520 U.S. counties and found that pediatric cases rose more sharply in plac-es that did not mandate masks in schools. A CDC press release on October 1 stated that in the two most populous counties in Arizona, schools without mask requirements were 3.5 times more likely to experience an outbreak than those with a mandate.

Texas school districts are required to report positive cases to the Texas Department of Health Services every Monday; these numbers were then posted each Friday. According to the collect-ed data, as reported by the *San Antonio Express-News* on October 11, NISD, our largest school district, which acted fast and required face masks from the start of the school year, had an infection rate of 1.8 percent. The next largest district, NEISD, which started with mandating face coverings and then reversed their policy, had a high infection rate of 3.7 percent.

The U.S. Department of Education began an investigation into Governor Abbott's ban on school mask mandates. The investigation focused on discrimination against students with disabilities, preventing them from safely attending school.

Locally, our hospital numbers continued to come down, declining to 705 by the following Sunday. But Texas still averaged 12,000 COVID-19 patients, with 284 daily deaths, one of the highest mortality rates in the nation.

On October 6, I gave my annual State of the County address to the Chamber of Commerce before a crowd of 500 people. It was great to get before a live audience. I said it was hard to understand that the three surges—summer of 2020, winter of 2020–21, and the current Delta surge—all went up for two months and then receded over two months. I stated it must be a combination of virus biology and human behavior.

I stated that the Delta surge was a crisis of the unvaccinated. Over 80 percent of those hospitalized were unvaccinated and over 95 percent of those COVID-19-related deaths were unvaccinated. I said that we were on the road to recovery, down from a high of 1,466 COVID 19 patients to 553 as of yesterday, but that the unvaccinated would continue to drive hospitalization. I went on to say that we need to invest and build to regain the lost momentum of economic development; I enumerated the many capital projects the city and county had underway.

I ended my speech by saying that 50 years ago this past January I had walked into the Texas House of Representatives as a freshman. That over the last 50 years I had served 32 years in public office as a state representative, state senator, San Antonio City Councilman, Mayor, and Bexar County Judge. I said I would serve out the remaining year and three months of my term and would not run for re-election. I thanked them for allowing me to serve my state, my city, and my county.

***

Throughout October, community health conditions continued to improve. Our media briefings were reduced to once a week on Tuesday as well as our conference calls with our team.

The FDA approved Pfizer's vaccine for children ages 5–11 for emergency on October 26. Vaccinating children would be a hard sell to parents, even though according to the CDC, nationwide approximately two million children ages 5–11 had been infected with COVID-19, 8,300 hospitalized, and least 170 had died.

According to a survey by the Kaiser Family Foundation, only about one in three families would allow their children to be vaccinated. On our media briefing, we encouraged parents to meet with their children's pediatrician.

On November 1 Commissioner Rodriguez and I visited the UHS Wonderland site as we began vaccinating children. When we arrived at 10:00 a.m. only a few parents and children were in line. We visited with parents and children and had pictures taken with them. By the time we left two hours later, the center was full of parents and children. Over 1,100 children were vaccinated. I was very happy at the turn out.

Mayor Nirenberg and I had a last media briefing on Tuesday, November 6. Our positivity rate was down below 2 percent. COVID-19 hospitalizations were at 161 from a high of 1,466 on August 23. We would continue to receive a daily situation report that we would examine to determine if there was any uptick in cases that would warrant a community warning.

On November 8, President Biden reopened our borders

to citizens from 33 countries, including European nations, provided they were vaccinated and had a negative COVID-19 test within three days of traveling. Our neighbors in Canada and Mexico could now cross the borders in vehicles as well as flights. Opening up our borders would have a positive impact on tourism, especially in our city where tourism is a major industry in our economy.

On the same day a report from the Texas Department of State Health Services was released that detailed the impact of the unvaccinated during the Delta surge. The data was collected from September 4 to October 1. It found that unvaccinated Texans were 20 times more likely to die from COVID-19 than the fully vaccinated. It also found that the unvaccinated were 13 times more likely to test positive from COVID-19.

The report also segmented age groups, finding that unvaccinated adults in their 40s were approximately two times more likely to die of COVID-19, while those over 75 were 12 times more likely to die. The unvaccinated made up nearly 92 percent of COVID-19 cases and 86 percent of deaths.

Our November 8 progress and warning indicator report showed that in the last week our positive test results were down to 1.5 percent, the lowest we had since the pandemic began. We were down to 140 COVID-19 patients in the hospital. Our overall risk level was low. Our fully vaccinated rate was 74.4 percent.

The social life of San Antonio began to open up. It seemed like every night a gala was underway. Tracy and I went to several evening events where hardly anyone wore a mask. The CDC had recommended that masks be worn when at indoor public events where community transmission of the virus was substantial or high. Our community was experiencing low transmission so those that were vaccinated felt confident not wearing a mask. With two shots and a booster, Tracy and I did not wear a mask at many events.

Tracy and I went to the Alamodome on November 20 to watch UTSA play University of Alabama at Birmingham, a football game for the Conference USA west division title. I joined University of Texas Regent Nolan Perez and UTSA President Taylor Eighmy on the field for the coin toss, which we won.

UTSA entered the game with a 10–0 record, ranking 22 in the top 25 teams in the nation. Over 35,000 fans cheered UTSA on to victory when quarterback Frank Harris threw a touchdown pass in the last three seconds of the game. It was an amazing victory for UTSA coach Jeff Traylor and his outstanding players. Two weeks later we went to the Conference USA finals and cheered on UTSA to a victory over Western Kentucky, our first conference championship.

So, life in Bexar County was back to normal. The economy was booming, and our hospitality industry had revived. We had a high vaccination rate of 74 percent, and our infection rate continued below 2 percent. School children infection rates had dramatically dropped.

But was it really finally over? Across the United States there were COVID-19 hot spots, particularly those with low vaccination rates. Similar hot spots were occurring in Europe. While we were concerned with hot spots, Mr. COVID decided it was time to rearm once again. He was not through with us, and we would quickly find out as Yogi Berra said, "It's not over till it's over."

9. Out of Africa—Omicron

THE WORLD HEALTH ORGANIZATION designated Omicron "a variant of concern" because of COVID-19's rearmament. With its power mutation, it had developed enhanced transmission. Dubbed Omicron, it made its way out of South Africa, crossed the ocean, and headed to the land of opportunity—especially in the southwest and southern states of America where the unvaccinated roamed.

Unlike the long delay in responding to the Delta variant that had originated in India, this time political leaders acted fast and imposed travel bans on November 26. But it was too late.

Two days later, on November 28, a traveler returning to San Francisco from Africa tested positive for COVID-19. Priority had been given to sequencing, and the results quickly determined that he had the Omicron variant. While we took notice, we continued life in a normal way, not knowing how serious to take this threat.

We felt more confident when the CDC said that the Pfizer and Moderna vaccines, reinforced with a booster, would provide significant protection against Omicron. Other shots, such as Johnson & Johnson, that did not use mRNA technology, offered less protection. Later studies from the U. K. Health Security Agency found that people who had two doses of vaccines were 65 percent less likely to be hospitalized and 81 percent less likely with three shots.

Researchers also found that Omicron had milder effects and was less likely to bind on lungs and therefore less likely to cause lower respiratory tract infections. But Omicron would prove to be a serious threat to the unvaccinated and those with underlying health issues.

***

Meanwhile as Christmas and New Year's Eve approached, people were moving around. For the first time in two years, Tracy and I boarded a plane and flew to New York on December 13 to join Commissioner Justin Rodriguez and County Manager David Smith to test the market to refinance and issue new county bonds. With the Delta variant still hovering around and the possible spread of Omicron, New York was taking no chances. What a different approach in culture and understanding of COVID-19 we found. Almost everywhere we went in New York, including restaurants, Broadway plays, offices, and museums, we had to provide our vaccination information. Regardless of where we were, we had to wear masks.

No wonder that Texas, with its "to hell with required health safety precautions" overtook New York in the number of COVID-19 deaths. As of December 27, according to USA FACTS there were 74,313 deaths in Texas compared to 58,911 in New York.

On Tuesday night Tracy and I attended a reception held at Henry and Mary Alice Cisneros' condo located on the East River. After the reception we had dinner in the club located in the condominium with Henry and Mary Alice and former CEO

and now Vice Chairman of Hearst Communications Corporation Board Frank A. Bennack, Jr. and his wife Mary Lake. Also
attending was Hearst Foundation Director George Irish and his
wife Jeanie and Jane Macon, our legal advisor on refinancing
bonds, and her husband Larry.

I had married Frank and Mary Lake 15 years earlier on
their ranch located in the Hill Country north of San Antonio. With
Henry's permission I had invited them to attend.

A lively conversation spun over a couple of hours with
Frank sharing with us his many memories of growing up in San
Antonio and his 20 years as CEO of the $11 billion, multilayered
media company that included our hometown newspaper, the *San
Antonio Express-News*. Henry spoke of his time in the cabinet
of President Bill Clinton as secretary of the U.S. Department of
Housing and Urban Development.

Tracy and I visited with Frank's wife Dr. Mary Lake Polan,
a professor of Clinical Obstetrics and Gynecology and Reproduc-
tive Sciences. We talked about the different approaches to containing COVID-19 and the breakthrough of mRNA vaccines. I told
her about my work on this book, and she said she was interested in
reading my latest draft, so I sent it to her.

Early each morning I ran in Central Park along with thousands of other people who were jogging, walking, riding bikes, and
chasing their dogs. In between daily bond meetings, I bought first
edition books at the Argosy and the Strand.

Tracy and I walked the streets enjoying the Christmas dec-
orations. We also attended a Broadway show, *Chicago*, where an
attendant held up a sign saying, "Put your mask on" as he searched
for any violators.

We ended the trip to New York on a good note when we

saved $42 million in interest by refinancing our bonds with a lower rate. We were able to receive a low interest rate because we were one of the few local governments that continued to have a Triple-A rating from all three of the major rating firms.

Back home we reinstituted our annual family baseball game on December 23, and then Tracy and I spent Christmas at home with my son, Matthew, his wife, Molly, and our two youngest grandchildren, Gideon and Madeline.

While our infection rate was only 2.2 percent before Christmas and we only had 200 COVID-19 patients in the hospital on Christmas Eve, we were beginning to see the first tell-tale signs that Omicron was beginning to spread in our community. It really hit home with me on December 27 when I arrived early at UHS hospital and took a seat in the emergency waiting room for an update on my daughter, Lynnie Slaughter, who had experienced COVID-19 symptoms. She was in great pain with a headache, fatigue, stomach cramps, and upper gastrointestinal complications.

As I sat waiting with my son-in-law Ronnie, UHS Medical Director Dr. Bryan Alsip stopped by to visit. He said that Omicron was spreading faster in one month than Delta did in four months. He said they were getting more and more Omicron patients over the last few days, and they expected the number to grow significantly. By the time that I left the emergency waiting room, it had grown from a few people to almost filling up; by the end of day it was standing room only.

The following day I returned to the hospital and found my daughter looking much better. While there I talked with Zahra Garza, an RN and executive director of the 10th floor, who told me that the increasing number of Omicron patients was occupying more beds in the hospital. After a few hours my daughter was released, and I took her home. She did not have COVID-19, but instead bacteria or another virus had infected her.

On December 29 it was reported by John Hopkins University that COVID-19 surged to a record of 265,000 cases per day nationwide eclipsing 250,000, a record set in January. On December 29, locally we had 325 COVID-19 hospital patients, an increase of 125 since Christmas Eve.

By now I was convinced that things were going to get a lot worse before they got better. Other than a video that Nirenberg and I had made advising everyone about the rapid rise of Omicron, we had not communicated with our citizens. Metro Health, during our conference call on December 29, stated that we should hold steady and not alarm people.

But I thought otherwise and called Nirenberg later and said that we needed to step up and tell citizens what we were experiencing in hospitals and our plan to handle what I believed would be a growing number of cases. I called UHS President George Hernandez, and he agreed to hold a press conference two days later on Friday, December 31.

On the morning of New Year's Eve, we held a press conference in the parking lot across from UHS hospital. I spoke first and related the visit I had with Dr. Alsip in the emergency room and my growing concern with a 77.7 percent increase in local COVID-19 hospitalizations in the last six days. I stated that the unvaccinated continued to drive hospitalization and said, "If you've got an unvaccinated friend, try to talk them into getting it—or stay the hell the way from them."

Dr. Alsip asked people not to go to the emergency room, but rather call their doctor. He said Omicron was exacerbating staffing challenges and that they were seeing an increase in the hospitalization of children. Across the nation children under five with COVID-19 reached the highest level since the pandemic began. Unvaccinated parents and others were endangering our youngest children.

Chief Nurse Executive Tommye Austin spoke of their staffing shortage and that citizens needed to implement safety protocols to help alleviate hospital stress. I then stated that we had asked the state for more nurses and that 411 were allocated to San Antonio, and we expected some to arrive next Monday.

Sheriff Javier Salazar stated that we had one inmate who had tested positive a few days ago, and now the jail had 38 positive inmates and 50 jail employees. COVID-19 was spreading fast, and he anticipated more cases in the jail. He announced that we would host a vaccination drive at the jail the following Tuesday.

Nirenberg cited that 80 percent of COVID-19 patients in the hospital were unvaccinated and emphasized the need for vaccinations as well as using health safety protocols. He also announced that several city COVID-19 testing sites were open.

We were right in sounding the alarm because by the following Monday our COVID-19 cases soared along with hospitalizations. We were averaging almost 4,000 cases a day, bringing our seven-day average to over 2,000 and a 27.3 percent positive infection rate—the highest since July 2020. Our COVID-19 hospitalizations rose to 506. Metro Health upgraded our overall risk level to "severe."

By now the CDC estimated that 90 percent of new COVID-19 cases in Texas were Omicron. We were able to obtain a new infusion monoclonal antibody, sotrovimab, that could be used to treat Omicron and hopefully prevent hospitalization. We had a limited supply, so under the National Institutes of Health's guidelines we only treated high-risk patients that were recommended by a doctor. National Institutes of Health is a department of HHS and is the largest biomedical research entity in the United States.

As an additional tool to ward off serious illness from COVID-19, the FDA authorized the Pfizer pill Paxlovid for those age 12 and older. The Merck pill molnupiravir was also authorized by the FDA for age 18 and older, but it was less effective than Paxlovid. A doctor's prescription is necessary for both pills. The FDA said a limited supply would be available in a few weeks.

As Omicron continued to spread, the demand for self-administered COVID-19 antigen tests intensified. Our priority was providing them for law enforcement, fire, and EMS personnel. The public could buy them in stores for about $20, but supplies were limited. President Biden promised everyone a late Christmas present of 500 million free rapid COVID-19 tests that were expected to arrive in early January.

Tracy and I had taken our first self-administered COVID-19 antigen test at home before Christmas to make sure we were safe before our grandchildren came over. It was easy to take with a nasal swab and a rapid result within 15 minutes. We both tested negative.

Former President Trump promoted vaccines in an interview and drew praise from President Biden. While coming late in the game, the endorsement helped. But still only 60 percent of Republicans had at least one shot as opposed to 91 percent of Democrats. Some 39 million Americans were still not vaccinated.

Two days after Christmas the CDC reduced the isolation time for those who had COVID-19 and were asymptomatic from ten to five days. Under the CDC's new guidelines if you were fully vaccinated and asymptomatic you did not have to quarantine if you were around someone with COVID-19, but you needed wear to a mask and be tested five to seven days after exposure. Data collected over the two years of the pandemic justified the new guidelines. But it did cause some confusion at the same time Omicron was spreading.

Meanwhile I had a controversial issue to deal with at the Commissioners Court. On December 13, Commissioner Trish De-Berry had announced she would run for county judge as a Republican. She would join three Democrats, former District Judge Peter Sakai, State Representative Ina Minjarez, and former Chief of Staff to Mayor Ron Nirenberg, Ivalis Meza Gonzalez, who were running to succeed me. DeBerry's announcement triggered an automatic resignation as soon as I appointed a new commissioner.

After reviewing 27 applicants, on Tuesday, January 4, I appointed former Republican Judge of the Fourth Court of Appeals Marialyn Barnard to take the place of DeBerry. Several of my fellow Democrats were not happy, as well as the 26 applicants I did not choose. But I believe in bipartisanship and Barnard was by far the best applicant. She had been a social worker, taught school, served as Assistant U.S. Attorney and CPS Energy corporate counsel, and served 10 years on the Fourth Court of Appeals.

Meanwhile Omicron was spreading up to seven times faster than the Delta variant, partly as the result of a lack of required safety protocols. Our hands had been tied behind our back by the overpowering state and Governor Abbott. All possible local mandatory health safety measures had been crushed by the governor. He stopped school requirements for face coverings and staff vaccinations. He issued an order prohibiting businesses to require weekly COVID-19 tests in lieu of vaccination. He sued to stop the National Guard from requiring vaccinations even though the military was required to do so. He prohibited us from restricting mass gatherings. We could not even require face coverings in government offices. We also could not require businesses to implement safety protocols. The pandemic, as seen by Abbott, was not about us but about himself as he fought off two right-wing Republicans in the primary.

We were in for a rough ride as COVID-19 hospitalizations continued to climb at a rapid rate. But how far would we spike up and then start to come down? UTSA professor of mathematics Juan Gutierrez predicted cases would continue to increase and then taper off by February—up and down fast—his model predicted. I hoped he was right.

Without authority to implement health safety protocols there were only five measures that we could take. First, Nirenberg and I needed to continue to communicate with our citizens. We needed to urge them to get vaccinated and adhere to health safety protocols. By the way, on my trips to H-E-B, I noticed that about 80 percent of the customers were wearing masks. Not too bad, but not good enough.

Second, and most important, was to keep our vaccine centers going. We continued to give shots at our Bexar County Hospital District mass vaccination center at Wonderland Mall five days a week from 8:00 a.m. to 6:00 p.m. We were averaging about 1,000 people a day including vaccinations for children. We had given 14,200 shots to children five and older.

Third, we needed to work with hospital CEOs to help them with staffing to meet the growing COVID-19 hospital patients. As you may recall, we were faced with a similar problem when the state waited two weeks to send more nurses. The Commissioners Court had set aside $5 million in case the state refused to help. I told STRAC Director Eric Epley that our funds were available if the hospitals needed the funding.

Fourth, we requested more sotrovimab monoclonal antibodies. We also sent a letter to Secretary of HHS Xavier Becerra asking for a supply of the antiviral drug remdesivir. We asked that it be sent to Regional Infusion centers in Texas, including our infusion center run by BCFS. Remdesivir would not be as effective as sotrovimab, but we only had a limited supply of only 3,000 a day issued to Texas.

Fifth, we needed to open more PCR COVID-19 testing sites because of the short supply of antigen test kits. On January 6 we opened a new city testing site at the headquarters of the Alamo College District. People were lined up around the building to be tested. Community Labs ran the testing site. People would get their results within 24 hours.

Five days later the Commissioners Court appropriated $1.3 million to open a testing site at our UHS Wonderland Mall mass vaccination site. It would be the only site in San Antonio offering mass vaccinations and testing.

On Sunday, January 9, I talked with Nirenberg and STRAC Director Eric Epley and urged both that we needed to get a letter off to Abbott requesting more nurses and technicians. By now we had 731 COVID-19 patients in the hospital, some of which were admitted for other aliments and tested positive for COVID-19.

Nationwide data showed that there would be no slowdown in the virus spread. Across the nation 145,982 COVID-19 patients were in the hospital including 4,462 children, breaking the previous peak on January 14, 2021.

We got the letter off Monday morning, and by the next day our hospitalization had grown to 889. A silver lining was that less patients were in ICU and on ventilators than in the Delta surge. I believe in large part you could attribute it to the work of Eric Epley, Director of STRAC. Throughout the pandemic he consulted with a team of infectious disease experts at each hospital and would update a shared information bulletin every two months, outlining the latest recommendations in the care of COVID-19 patients.

All the stories written about Omicron causing only mild symptoms caused people to be less careful. Studies had shown that Omicron infected the upper respiratory tract rather than lung tissue, resulting in it being as not as dangerous as Delta. While the statement was true in most cases, the sheer number of cases would result in many cases where Omicron was in fact dangerous, particularly in people with existing health conditions.

As COVID-19 mutated, the structure of the virus changed, and vaccines became somewhat less effective. While vaccinated patients in our hospitals were now at 30 percent, they were not headed to intensive care. A study published in *The New England Journal of Medicine* revealed that 98 percent of those receiving a Pfizer vaccine prevented the need for intensive care and life support.

As Omicron spread, we were reaching what some people called herd immunity. We would soon run out of people to infect, and that is why predictions were that we would see a steep rise and steep fall. By January 15 we began to see a fall of cases in New York and New Jersey. But even when we would begin a downward slope, many people would still end up in the hospital.

On Wednesday, January 12, Nirenberg and I had a WebEx meeting with all the school district superintendents. All 15 districts were implementing weekly COVID-19 tests, sanitizing school rooms, controlling crowding in hallways, and strongly encouraging face coverings.

SAISD had the most comprehensive program. Interim Superintendent Robert Jaklich (Pedro Martinez had resigned to become superintendent of the Chicago School System) appointed a team headed up by Toni Thompson to implement mandatory safety protocols—in some cases ignoring Governor Abbott's emergency orders. They had a mask mandate and provided volunteer weekly testing for all students as well as contact tracing. Those involved in extracurricular activities were required to take COVID-19 tests. They created a mobile testing unit and hosted 90 vaccination clinics. Because of their strong health protocols, they had a lower percentage of positive cases than the other school districts.

On Friday, December 14 we opened a testing site on the first floor of the Wonderland Mall with funds passed by the Commissioners Court the previous week. Community Labs ran the testing site. We continued to give vaccinations on the second floor administered by our Bexar County Hospital District.

Nirenberg and I attended the opening day and spoke while people seeking the tests were lined up behind us. We encouraged teenagers to be tested and vaccinated. Nationwide, according to the CDC, only 36 percent of children ages 12–17 had been vaccinated and nearly all the teenagers in the hospital had not been vaccinated.

Afterwards we went to the South Texas Blood Bank where we spoke of the need for people to donate blood. Our blood supply was down to one day, whereas normally we had a seven-day supply.

We then took a tour of Community Lab's testing site located in the building. CEO Sal Webber told us that over $2.5 million was invested in the state-of-the-art PCR testing equipment. The process is complicated, requiring some seven different steps. That is why PCR tests are more reliable, but at the same time it takes longer to get results.

On the same day the U. S. Supreme Court struck down President Biden's order to impose mandatory testing for businesses employing over 100 workers. Texas businesses were caught in a vice between Biden's order and Governor Abbott's order that the employers had no right to demand vaccinations. Biden and Abbott should have left employers alone and let them decide what they wanted to do.

I found it interesting to contrast the western world with China, a country that had resorted to massive shutdowns and stay-at-home orders to control the virus. It began with the city of Wuhan (12 million people) where the virus first emerged in early 2020. Now in January 2022 the city of Xi'an (13 million people) was shut down after Omicron began to spread. With the fast-spreading Omicron it was doubtful their strategy would continue to work.

China's "Zero-COVID-19" strategy, while successful in holding down infections, was taking a huge toll on their economy and the health of their citizens. I believe we were right in shutting down only when our hospitals were in severe condition, but many states were wrong in stopping mandatory health protocols. The Republican governor's hands-off strategy resulted in numerous people entering the hospitals and some dying.

But the Republican COVID-19 strategy gained popularity as Trump emerged as the most powerful Republican figure. It turned out that after his social media platform was banned from posting his lies and distortions, he became more popular. His unfavourability rating dropped from a 20-point spread to a nine-point gap according to FiveThirtyEight's average of national polls. He was his own worst enemy, and now with most of his mouth covered up, he emerged as a more powerful voice, resulting in the Republican party declaring on February 4 that the January 6, 2021, attack on our capitol was a "legitimate political discourse." How terribly sad.

Partly as a result of Trump and the governor trashing required health safety protocols, Omicron took off in our community sending many of the unvaccinated to the hospital and some dying.

Metro Health Assistant Director Dr. Anita Kurian reported to us on that the Omicron variant fueled a blizzard like we have never seen before in the previous three surges. We had 326 positive cases on December 13. She said that within a four week span our seven-day average climbed to 6,795 cases. In a comparison to our highest previous surge, we had an average of 2,437 positive cases, a 4,358 difference between the peaks. As the cases continued to climb so did our hospitalization. From 203 COVID-19 patients on December 13, four weeks later we had 1,028 COVID-19 on January 14.

We continued our successful vaccination sites. As of January 15, the state had a vaccination rate of 61.8 percent compared to our 72.4 percent. We were also doing better than the four other large counties. But unfortunately, only 27 percent of our citizens got a booster shot. The failure to get a booster shot led to many more infections and hospitalizations because the effectiveness of vaccines decline as time passes.

Unlike the previous four surges, people entered the hospital because of other health issues, then tested positive for Omicron because it was so widespread. Nationwide studies showed an average of 40 to 50 percent of COVID-19 patients entered the hospital for other health issues. Most had mild COVID-19 symptoms or none at all.

According to the CDC, 13 percent of Omicron hospital patients ended up in the ICU as opposed to 18 percent of the earlier surges of COVID-19. Nationwide the Omicron surge was causing 2,191 COVID-19 deaths each day, exceeding the Delta surge. Total COVID-19 deaths in the United States since the pandemic started reached 900,000 on February 4, exceeding the population of San Francisco. John Hopkins University, where the data was complied, predicted that by April we would have one million deaths. On that same day we reached a local total of 5,135 COVID-19 deaths. WHO estimates that 5, 705,754 people worldwide have died from COVID-19 as of the same date.

As unvaccinated deaths continued to rise, on February 5 President Biden made a special plea for everyone to get vaccinated. He estimated that one million lives had been saved by the vaccine. Based on a study in November 2021, the CDC estimated that unvaccinated people were more than 53 times more likely to die from COVID-19 than those who were vaccinated and had their booster shot.

After hitting a high of 1,308 COVID-19 patients in the hospital on January 26 our numbers began to fall. By March 13, we were down to 159 COVID-19 patients.

Our positivity rate dropped to 4.9 percent from a high of over 30 percent. Our overall risk level dropped to mild from a high of severe.

Nirenberg and I felt confident that the worst was over and we would now be able to manage COVID-19. We also know variants can continue to evolve, such as the BA.2 Omicron subvariant that was slightly more transmissible. UHS epidemiologist Dr. Jason Bowling stated that we will continue to see COVID-19 variants around for a long time. Some experts bellieve that we will have to learn to live it with as it prowls around much like the flu, requiring annual vaccinations. Others warn that a new more dangerous variant may emerge.

We must be ready for whatever comes our way.

10. The Coming of the Unborn Virus

AS THIS BOOK GOES TO PRESS, approximately 25 percent of Bexar County's population has tested positive for COVID-19. Over 40,000 of our citizens have been hospitalized over the two-year pandemic. Tragically 5,295 of our citizens have died from COVID-19.

Due in part to the stripping away of health safety protocols by the governor, 83,549 people in the state have died from COVID-19. We almost exceeded California's 84,381 deaths—a state with 10 million more citizens.

Since the COVID-19 pandemic began in early 2020, Mayor Nirenberg and I have participated in 349 daily conference calls with health officials and reviewed 594 COVID-19 daily situation reports. From that information we held 319 daily COVID-19 media briefings where we shared with our citizens the current status of COVID-19, the 30 emergency orders that we enacted, and our advice on health safety protocols.

Throughout the pandemic Mayor Nirenberg and I said numerous times how important it was for all our citizens to follow health safety protocols. Nirenberg would end our media briefing with a plea: "Do it for yourself, do it for your family. Do it for San Antonio."

The vast majority of Bexar County's two million citizens followed our advice, showing a respect for each other. The overarching philosophical principle was that we were in this together and together we would manage the COVID-19 crisis. I believe that philosophy will carry over into a more caring, thoughtful society in all the future issues we may deal with in our community.

We realize that the future of the virus is still uncertain, but whatever the future may be, we will be ready. Our understanding of the virus has taken a quantum leap over the last two years, giving us new advances in medicine, treatment, and prevention.

As we move forward in managing COVID-19, as well as preparing for the coming of the unborn virus that will surely emerge, I have a few observations and recommendations to share with you. The first nine observations and thoughts are on how we should prepare for future pandemics, and the last three are on how we should strengthen our economy through inspiring and preparing our workforce for the future.

1. Develop an infectious disease plan and restructure agencies to carry it out.

President Trump trashed a 69-page plan developed by the Obama administration that would provide an early response to high-consequence emerging infectious disease threats and biological incidents. Not only did he disregard the report, but he also dismantled the pandemic response team. His early actions contributed to a chaotic response to the pandemic that led to loss of lives.

President Biden and future presidents should implement changes to the playbook based on what we learned from the pandemic and have a team ready to respond to the next threat. An integral part of that plan will be developing new leadership and structure for the CDC that will enable the agency to plan for a quick, effective intervention in the next pandemic.

With offices and staff all over the world, we also need to be involved with WHO in developing an agreement between all nations to immediately respond and communicate their knowledge about any evolution of new viruses that could lead to a pandemic. China was slow to communicate the threats of COVID-19.

We should also support an independent panel that found that WHO must be restructured and staffed adequately in order to implement a worldwide response to any future pandemic. At the same time, local communities must also be prepared. We are working on local plans that will provide a more unified approach to any future pandemic as recommended in observation nine.

2. When facing a virus threat, act first with genome sequencing, comprehensive testing, and contact tracing.

First, prompt genome sequencing is necessary to identify the virus early on and take steps to manage it. At the onset of the pandemic, China withheld information, making it difficult to identify the virus.

We got it right with the emergence of Omicron. When a traveler returning to San Francisco from Africa on November 28, 2021, tested positive for COVID-19, priority was given to sequencing, and the results quickly determined that he had the Omicron variant. That information enabled us to quickly develop sotrovimab, a monoclonal antibody treatment for Omicron.

Second, we must develop a prompt, accurate testing system. The CDC was slow in rolling out COVID-19 test kits that could be used to detect, track, and slow the spread of COVID-19.

The CDC made a mistake by choosing to not accept a German test that had been approved by WHO. Instead, they decided to create their own test and ran into design flaws and contamination when they began developing tests kits. They also made it difficult for laboratories to design their own tests.

Once we finally received testing kits, we ran into problems when labs took as long as four days to deliver the results of the tests. To get quicker results, a local non-profit organization, Community Labs, opened a local testing lab that produced results in 14 hours. Testing is now easier after the FDA approved two rapid at-home COVID-19 antigen tests. But again, we had supply problems. With the fast-spreading Omicron, stores ran out of supplies.

Third, we must be ready to implement contact tracing. Locally we were slow in ramping up, but once we did, contact tracing saved numerous lives by providing information that enabled infected people to isolate and people in close contact to quarantine. In the future we must be much better prepared for genome sequencing, comprehensive testing, results, and contact tracing.

3. Don't shut down businesses—instead mandate business health safety protocols, control gatherings, and prepare hospitals to handle the next pandemic.

Our "Stay Home, Work Safe" order was necessary because our hospital systems were not prepared for an influx of COVID-19 patients. But the shutdown had a devastating impact on our economy and the mental stress of our citizens.

COVID-19 lockdowns resulted in isolation, loss of jobs, and along with other factors, led to mental stress and higher use of dangerous drugs. People dying from an overdose of drugs soared to 100,000 in the 12-month period ending in April 2021, according to the National Center for Health Statistics. It eclipsed the previous year's deaths by almost 30 percent.

We should never have to shut down businesses locally again because our hospitals are now prepared to handle COVID-19 patients. They now have an adequate stock of PPE and have developed new medicines and medical procedures that reduces time spent in the hospital.

We have now gone through four major surges of COVID-19 where hospitals have learned to staff up with temporary nurses. We are also increasing the number of hospitals. Locally we have two new hospitals under construction and two in the planning stage.

Second, mayors and county judges should have the authority to mandate safety protocols for businesses such as spacing, face mask mandates, sanitation, PPE, clothing, and new building codes requiring fresh air circulation. We implemented mandatory safety protocols for businesses in June of 2020, and it proved to be very effective. Unfortunately, many months later Governor Abbott struck down mandatory business safety protocols.

Third, mayors and county judges should have the authority to ban large gatherings of people. We learned through the pandemic that large gatherings are super-spreaders of COVID-19. Early in the pandemic we saw the effect of the New Orleans Mardi Gras celebrations where thousands of people became infected with COVID-19.

Georgia Tech researchers found that on average, if 25 people gathered there was a 68 percent probability of someone having COVID and 90 percent if 100 or more gather.

4. Closing K-12 public schools should be a last resort.

When Governor Abbott closed schools in 2020, it led

to issues of inequality in technology, breakfast and school lunch programs, and educational achievement. The closing also placed a huge burden upon families as they scrambled to find childcare facilities and somehow handle their older children. In many cases their children were at greater risk of contracting COVID-19 than if they had been in school. Instead of closing, schools should enact health safety protocols.

First, school officials should enhance their buildings to help protect inhabitants from any viruses now or in the future. Schools need to install UV lamps on both sides of where air enters and exits the air vents. They should deploy HEPA scrubbing machines in congregate settings and high traffic locations and adjust HVAC controls to increase the air changes per hour in the building to an average of four to six. These are all good health safety issues to take even without the threat of a pandemic.

Second, school officials should have the authority to require masks, spacing, staggering classes, and most importantly, periodic COVID-19 testing. Our local school districts were successful during the Omicron surge when they instituted required health safety protocols.

Our lawsuit against Governor Abbott provided cover for schools to ignore his order that restricted their rights. For example, SAISD and NISD mandated face coverings and required COVID-19 testing for those in extracurricular activities. All districts provided volunteer weekly testing for all students as well as contact tracing. Many created a mobile testing unit and hosted vaccination clinics.

Third, schools should also offer remote learning for those students who have parental support and good digital connections. A top priority for the future must be breaking the digital divide.

An internet connection should be viewed as a public utility, much like electrical, gas, and water. New legislation by the U.S. Congress must be passed to create digital access for all homes. Mayor Nirenberg and I are moving forward on a local plan, with significant help from the federal government, to lay backbone cable through the county enabling every home to be connected.

5. Grant private and public employers the right to require vaccinations or weekly virus testing.

Too many of our citizens refused to be vaccinated resulting in the unvaccinated surge of Delta and Omicron. Approximately 75 percent of our COVID-19 hospital patients were unvaccinated and over 90 percent of deaths were unvaccinated. They will drive up medical costs for all of us when insurance companies seek rate increases. In addition to hospital costs, the fusion treatments they took were 10 times the cost of vaccines.

Many employers have voluntarily stepped up to require vaccinations for all employees except for those who have a health condition. Some required weekly tests for the unvaccinated, limited them to certain areas, and imposed a health care surcharge.

Governor Abbott issued an emergency order on October 10, 2021, that banned any employer in Texas from requiring vaccinations for employees or customers. He was trampling on the rights of employers to protect their own employees. Federal and state legislation needs to be passed granting employers the authority to mandate vaccinations or offer alternative restrictions to the unvaccinated.

6. Limit the governor's authority to suspend local orders that would prevent, hinder, or delay necessary local action in coping with a disaster.

During the pandemic, Mayor Nirenberg and I enacted 30 emergency orders based on science and health officials' advice. The emergency orders included face mask mandates, limited gatherings, curfews, business safety protocols, and other health safety issues. These actions were evidence-based and necessary to fight the spread of COVID-19.

County judges and city mayors in all six major counties of Texas that make up 51 percent of the Texas population issued similar orders. Collectively our emergency orders provided safety protocols to protect our citizens and were effective until the governor's emergency orders stripped local officials of the right to cope with the COVID-19 pandemic.

Early in the pandemic, Governor Abbott recognized the right of local officials to enact public safety mandates beyond his emergency orders, but as the pandemic progressed, he gave into political pressure and enacted emergency orders that tied our hands.

Legislation needs to be passed in Texas and other states that clearly identifies the power of local officials and the governor. The governor's authority should be limited to suspending local orders that would in any way prevent, hinder, or delay necessary local action in coping with a disaster.

7. Pass legislation that requires social media companies to control messages of hate and misinformation.

During the pandemic the most dangerous social media postings were related to false information about vaccines. We worked hard to overcome these irrational voices, but many citizens had bought into the misinformation posted on social media. Matters became worse when politicians sought to stop responsible steps taken by the computer and communication industries to restrict the misinformation and toxic messages. The Texas legislature passed legislation to allow the lies and misinformation to continue. Under the Texas law, Facebook, Twitter, and other social media firms were denied their First Amendment right to determine the content published on their platforms.

A federal judge stopped the implementation of the legislation on December 2. It is now being appealed. The United States Supreme Court should act to protect the First Amendment rights of social media firms to control their content.

Congress must mandate that social media firms institute a much better system of flagging and deleting false information and hate messages. People that have been harmed should have rights to sue social media firms as well as class actions against the social media companies.

8. Ramp up research to create new virus medicines and vaccines.

The vaccines developed during the COVID-19 pandemic ushered in a new era of vaccinology. A Yale University and Commonwealth Fund study released in July 2021 found that these vaccines had prevented 1.25 million from being hospitalized and 279,000 deaths.

The mRNA technology that was used to develop the COVID-19 vaccine has the potential for medical applications beyond COVID-19. According to a *Wall Street Journal* report, venture capitalists are funding mRNA start-ups.

At the same time Pfizer, Merck, Moderna, and other pharmaceutical companies are investing more funds in technology to enhance mRNA technology. Biotech has 21 mRNA products under development that use 11 different means to kill cancer cells. They also published a study that found an mRNA vaccine has the potential to treat multiple sclerosis.

The pandemic also led to the development of new medicines. The development of monoclonal antibody treatments for high-risk patients who were ill with COVID-19 was successful. We opened an infusion center that provided antibodies through infusions to over 10,000 patients. Merck, Ridgeback Biotherapeutics, and Pfizer have now developed antiviral pills that can be taken instead of an infusion.

Additional federal dollars should be allocated to the National Institutes of Health, the largest biomedical research entity in the United States, as well as independent research labs such Texas Biomedical Research Institute, located in our community.

9. Align public health and medical and hospital care to set comprehensive health care objectives that include health equity, acute care, preventive care, and pandemic response.

During the pandemic UHS ran the largest and most efficient mass COVID-19 vaccination in Texas, administering over 500,000 doses of the vaccine at Wonderland Mall. They also hosted a COVID-19 testing site at the same site. They have treated hundreds of COVID-19 patients in their hospital. But they had virtually no say in public health policies and decisions. With the experience UHS gained during the pandemic, they should be on the front line of public health decisions.

UHS has more than 9,000 employees and an annual budget of $2.5 billion. The UHS hospital has the most specialized and advanced services for complex illnesses and injuries in all major specialties. As a teaching hospital they have a partnership with UT Health San Antonio and a comprehensive team of doctors, nurses, technicians, researchers, and virus experts.

In addition to the 2-million sq. ft. state-of-the-art hospital, they also operate three Express-Med urgent care centers, 25 outpatient care centers, two outpatient surgery centers, four outpatient renal dialysis centers, and a world-class center for diabetes research and education. They are expanding telemedicine, hospital-at-home, digitizing all patient medical records, building a new state-of-the-art Women and Children's Hospital, and have purchased three sites for new hospitals. They have won numerous awards and recognition nationwide, like Chime's Most Wired for Acute and Ambulatory Digital Health. In 2021 only nine U.S. health systems have reached this level of expertise.

The COVID-19 pandemic showed how a virus can trigger a quick reaction in people with preexisting serious health issues that often results in immediate sickness or death, robbing them of many years of life. Over 40,000 COVID-19 patients have entered our local hospitals over the last two years. Almost all of the over 5,000 COVID-19 deaths were people with underlying health issues such as obesity, diabetes, hypertension, and chronic kidney and liver conditions.

On March 15, 2022, all five members of the Commissioners Court held a press conference, along with UHS officials, and announced that UHS would create a public health division. The Commissioners Court would provide up to $60 million in funding to build a new headquarters for UHS Public Health, to be located next to Texas A&M University on the south side of San Antonio. A nine-member advisory committee appointed by the Commissioners Court and UHS Board of Managers would be established.

Bringing UHS resources to the table will strengthen public health initiatives, improve health equity, and provide a comprehensive approach to preventive care, acute care, and pandemic response.

10. Prepare our workforce and small businesses for the future.

The national economy began to rebound in May 2021, reaching close to the pre-pandemic levels in October. As of January 22, 2022, our unemployment rate in Bexar County was only 3.6 percent as opposed to 4.3 percent in the state of Texas. We added 49,000 jobs in the past year.

Because of the strong economic rebound, there are more job openings than workers. Many people decided to drop out of the workforce either through early retirement or other reasons. For example, in September 2021 a record 4.4 million workers quit their jobs according to the U.S. Bureau of Labor Statistics. As a result, wages have gone up and new job opportunities have opened.

Critical to the success of our changing workforce are job-training programs that recognize the skills necessary for well-paying technology-related work. Locally, we are focusing on job-training programs related to advanced manufacturing, health care, cybersecurity, arts, construction, and back-office support. Mayor Ron Nirenberg led the effort to convince voters to approve $174 million in funding to create new job-training programs. Over 40,000 people will be offered training.

Because we have a fast-growing manufacturing industry, Bexar County is concentrating on training for advanced manufacturing jobs. We are building a new training center in a partnership with private employers to train for new skills including data analyzing, design thinking, prescriptive maintenance practices, technology evolution, and general problem solving.

The pandemic also stirred up a new era of entrepreneurship. As people adjusted to working over the internet, they found new opportunities as they improved their social media and computer skills. They had the opportunity to use apps and visit websites that cater to small businesses, giving them a chance to become an entrepreneur. As a result, a historic number of people chose to become self-employed. According to *The Wall Street Journal*, 4.54 million new businesses were registered from January through October of 2021, an increase of 56 percent above the same period in the pre-pandemic year of 2019.

Small businesses are a driving force in creating jobs. Over the years we have taken the lead in supporting small businesses. Bexar County Small Business Director Renee Watson started a small business conference in 2002, my second year as county judge. Since then, we have attracted over 70,000 entrepreneurs.

In Bexar County we had over a 25 percent increase in new startups in 2021. As a result, we stepped up outreach efforts to startups after the Commissioners Court provided additional funding to increase staff. During the pandemic we provided $20 million to small businesses to enable them through the tough years.

11. Expand flexible work to give employees choices of where and how to work.

Companies and employees have learned that working from home is mutually beneficial. Working at home saves travel expenses and food cost and allows closer family contact. Work productivity increases with less office-related interruptions.

Spending more time together during the pandemic strengthened families. A nation is built on the strength of stable, productive families giving children parental time and nourishment that prepares them for the future. Hopefully the impact will be long term as families recognize the benefits of sharing time with each other.

According to an American Family Survey of 3,000 adults,

conducted by the Brigham Young University, marriages in trouble fell from 40 percent in 2019 to 29 percent during 2020. Divorce rates went down.

Bexar County built a new state-of-the-art Information Technology office that provides workers with mobility choice. We reduced space requirements down to handle only one-third of our workforce, with the remaining two-thirds working from home. Every employee has a laptop and an available shared workstation in the office. Many other companies are following suit.

Increased skills of workers are needed along with expanded technology to allow more workers the choice to work from home or split their work between office and home.

12. Congress should enact a comprehensive immigration policy that would expand our workforce.

Hearst newspapers examined the U.S. Department of Health and Human Services' data on all deaths in 2020, the first year of pandemic, and found that deaths from any cause jumped 22 percent. It was the largest single-year increase in over 50 years tracking back to 1964, the first year of reliable data. Deaths from 1964–2019 increased annually by only 2 percent.

As a result of the pandemic, life expectancy in the United States fell by 1.5 years in 2020 to 77.3 years, according to an article in *The Wall Street Journal* on July 21, 2021. It was the biggest decline since World War II.

Immigration counts for between a third and a half of the population growth in the past decade. With a population growth rate projected at only 0.35 percent, increased immigration will be critical to expand our workforce. If we are not successful, jobs will move to countries with an expanding workforce.

Many congressmen and senators on both sides of the isle demonize immigrants. When immigrants seeking asylum cross the Texas border, they are met by the National Guard and hauled off to jail under orders of Governor Abbott. Immigrants who have been in our country for years have no pathway to citizenship.

Congressmen and senators continue to block a new immigration policy that would build a pathway to citizenship and allow additional work permits. Unless Congress comes to terms and enacts a new immigration policy, our economy will begin a decline and along with it jobs.

***

I feel confident that the institutions of science, technology, and medicine will continue to successfully manage Omicron as well as future virus pandemics. But I have serious reservations about how our politicians and citizens will respond to their advice and leadership in any future pandemic.

The last two years of the pandemic—well actually a little longer—have brought out the worst in human behavior. The foundation for this craziness was laid by President Trump when he became the champion of using social media to create mangled, alternative facts and outright lies. The more the lies are repeated over social media, the more people began to accept them as the truth.

Researchers at Massachusetts Institute of Technology in 2018 found that false stories on Twitter travel six times faster than truth and reach a lot more people. This does not count false stories from bots and cyborgs.

Trump also recognized his own emotions and those of others. He understood the power of emotional intelligence (EI) in how it could guide human behavior. Many experts believe that

EI is twice as important as IQ. Trump understood that you must motivate, provoke, urge action, and be energetic and confident by using the most powerful emotion—fear. In a political showdown such as the pandemic, EI carried the day over IQ.

Trump's knowledge was passed on to thousands of his supporters, and many of them became proficient in deploying his tactics. As a result, the information age has become the disinformation age, leading to an unraveling of truth and a polarization as human vulnerability. The abnormal becomes the normal in a nation that is going a little crazy.

During the pandemic, a barrage of attacks were launched on the principles of reason, rational behavior, positive attitudes, ethical behavior, and respect for each other that are critical to the functioning of our society. The pandemic also threw into doubt our trusted institutions of public education, medicine, science, mass media, and democracy. These institutions shaped our thoughts and behavior as we strove for positive civic engagement.

Some 40 million people chose not to be vaccinated even though medical professionals assured them the vaccine was effective and safe. People and politicians ignored medical advice regarding required health safety protocols. As a result of the attacks, COVID-19 spread faster and drove up the number of people requiring hospitalization, with many people dying.

President Trump's false election claims and the attack on our capitol on January 6 came close to destroying our democracy. Our free and independent national media came under attack. A large majority of our population chose to rely on sources from social media who spread false information and buried the truth.

Truth gets lost when fabricated and distorted facts are repeated and become accepted as true. The public does not know what to believe when numerous mangled facts are presented as true facts. Mix a little fear with partial truth and the demagogue prevails.

As a *New York Times* editorial stated, "Truth is hard. Truth must be pursued. Truth cannot be manufactured. Truth is powerful. Truth is under attack. Truth is worth defending. Truth is more important than ever."

While truth is under attack it can still be powerful if you fight back, pounding away on true facts and refuting the half-truths and lies. Because false stories spread faster than wind-blown seeds, no matter how hard you push truth, it is subject to wins and losses.

Somehow, we have to come to our senses if we are going to prepare our citizens for any future pandemic. Hopefully as time passes and we reflect back on the pandemic, maybe everybody will finally realize that it should have been about us working together following science and public health standards.

And maybe once we realize that the pandemic should have been about us, we can take that lesson forward and create a national dialogue on preparation for any future pandemics as well as other issues.

That's my hope.

History of COVID-19 Patients in San Antonio Area Hospitals

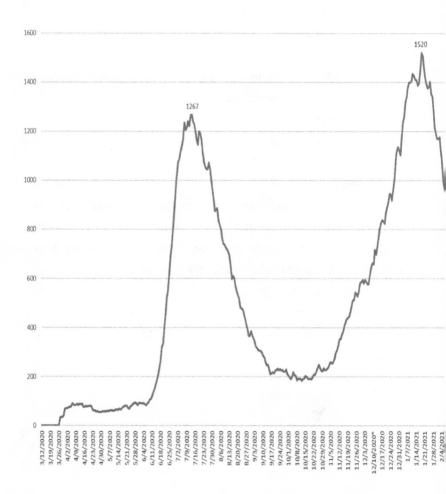

03/12/2020–02/10/2022

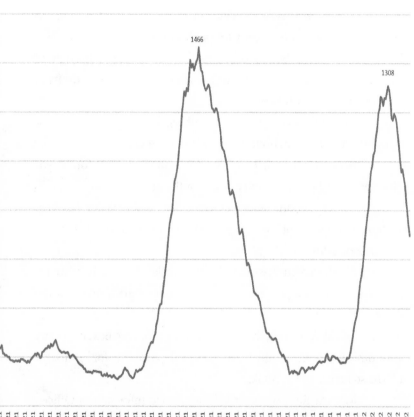

Acknowledgments

I first want to thank Mick and Diane Prodger at Elm Grove Publishing for publishing this book and providing great insight on the topics I have written about.

Nancy Mathews, my editor, for doing an outstanding job getting the finished book ready for publication.

My Chief of Staff Nicole Erfurth for her support throughout the COVID-19 pandemic and for her review of numerous drafts of the book and help with corrections.

San Antonio Mayor Ron Nirenberg for the foreword and for our partnership throughout the COVID-19 pandemic.

Bruce Davidson, Director of Communications for Mayor Nirenberg, for his review and critique of the book.

My Communications Director James Rivera for his help with tech-support during the COVID-19 pandemic and his review of numerous drafts of the book.

My Research Assistant Evan Viroslav for his help in researching various topics and his review of numerous drafts of the book.

David Marquez, Executive Director of the Bexar County Economic and Community Development department, for his insight on the structure of the book.

Monica Ramos, Bexar County Public Information Officer, for her tireless work to keep the public informed about Commissioners Court decisions regarding health and safety precautions during the COVID-19 pandemic and her advice on the book.

University Health System President George Hernandez for his support throughout the COVID-19 pandemic and his review of the book. University Health System Vice President Leni Kirkman for editing UHS sections of the book.

Dr. Barbara Taylor, Infectious Disease Specialist with the UT Health System, for her insight on the development of the mRNA vaccine.

References and Sources

The Advocate

American Academy of Family Physicians

American Society of Nephrology

The Associated Press

The Associated Press-NORC Center for Public Affairs Research

Axios News

Axios-Ipsos Coronavirus Index

Bexar Facts polls

Bexar County Office of Emergency Management

Bexar County Public Information Office

Cell Reports; "High-affinity memory B cells induced by SARS-CoV-2 infection produce more plasmablasts and atypical memory B cells than those primed by mRNA vaccines." https://www.cell.com/cell-reports/fulltext/S2211-1247(21)01287-0?_returnURL=https%3A%2F%2Flinkinghub.elsevier.com %2Fretrieve%2Fpii%2FS2211124721012870%3Fshowall%3Dtrue

Centers for Disease Control and Prevention (CDC)

CDC; "Implementation and Evolution of Mitigation Measures, Testing, and Contact Tracing in the National Football League, August 9–November 21, 2020." https://www.cdc.gov/mmwr/volumes/70/wr/mm7004e2.htm?s_cid=mm7004e2_w

Center for Countering Digital Hate

Cleveland Clinic

Code Breaker by Walter Isaacson

Daily Beast

Federal Aviation Administration

Georgia Institute of Technology; "The COVID-19 Event Risk Assessment Planning Tool." https://covid19risk.biosci.gatech.edu/

Houston Chronicle

Imperial College of London; "Public risk perceptions and behavioral responses during COVID-19." https://www.imperial.ac.uk/patient-experience-research-centre/covid-19/covid-19-research/risk-behaviour/

International Computer Science Institute

Kaiser Family Foundation

Kaiser Permanente

Los Angeles Times

National Geographic

National Institutes of Health

National Library of Medicine

National Nurses United

Nature magazine

The New York Times

PLOS One; "Safe reopening on college campuses during COVID-19: The University of California experience in Fall 2020." https://journals.plos.org/plosone/article?id=10.1371/journal.pone.0258738

POLITICO

Proceedings of the National Academy of Sciences of the United States of America; "An evidence review of face masks against COVID-19." https://pubmed.ncbi.nlm.nih.gov/33431650/

RAND Corporation

San Antonio Express-News

San Antonio Metropolitan Health District

San Antonio Report

Scientific American

Southwest Texas Regional Advisory Council (STRAC)

Texas Department of State Health Services

Texas Education Agency (TEA)

Texas Monthly magazine

The Texas Politics Project

Texas State Historical Association

The Texas Tribune

Time magazine

Timeanddate.com

U.S. Bureau of Labor Statistics

U.S. Department of Health and Human Services

U.S. Department of the Treasury

U.S. Food and Drug Administration (FDA)

University Health System (UHS)

University of Texas Health Science Center at San Antonio (UT Health)
University of Texas at San Antonio (UTSA) Department of Mathematics
The Wall Street Journal
The Washington Post
Willis Towers Watson
World Health Organization (WHO)
Yale Medicine
Yale School of Public Health

Index

Abbott, Greg *34, 35, 37, 38, 41, 45, 55, 58, 60-63, 65, 70, 76, 77, 79, 82, 84, 86, 89, 91, 93-95, 108, 111, 115, 141, 147, 148, 152, 156, 161, 162, 167, 170, 176-178, 180, 183, 184, 187-201, 203, 204, 211-214, 220*

Abbott Lab BinaxNOW test *149*

AirLIFE *123*

Alamo Heights Independent School District (AHISD) *120, 180*

Alamo Museum *148, 160*

Alamo Plaza *72, 73, 148*

Alamodome *33, 34, 86, 132, 140, 164, 191*

Alsip, Dr. Brian *37, 130, 145, 157, 196*

American Basketball Association (ABA) *33*

American Rescue Plan Act (ARPA) *159, 160*

Andrews, Jada *69*

Angry Elephant bar *117*

Archer, Christian *77, 79*

Army North *88, 167, 168*

Arndt, Jeff *45*

Arteaga, Judge Antonia *174, 177, 178*

Associated Press *156, 166*

Audie Murphy Memorial VA Hospital *25*

Austin, Lloyd *180*

Axious/Ipsos *178*

Azar, Alex *26*

B & B Smoke House *109*

Bakke, Phil *67, 106, 148*

Bamlanivimab *117*

Baptist Health System *25*

Barcus, Sara *13, 87, 88*

Battelle Mask Decontamination site *60*

BCFS *117, 201*

Bean, Judge Roy *82*

Becerra, Xavier *201*

Bellaire High School *133*

Bellaire Varsity Club *133*

Berggren, Dr. Ruth *37, 57, 157*

Berra, Yogi *70, 191*

Bexar County *10, 21, 23, 24, 28-30, 37, 38, 40, 46, 48, 49, 51, 53, 56, 59, 65-67, 73, 74, 84, 85, 90, 91, 100, 107, 109, 113, 125, 126, 128, 138, 148, 150, 151, 153, 154, 156, 157, 159, 160, 164, 169, 173, 174, 183, 188, 191, 208, 217-219*

Bexar County Commissioners Court *24, 30, 31, 37, 42, 45, 46, 51, 57, 65, 79, 85, 97, 101, 103, 111, 112, 114, 118, 119, 122, 126, 130, 135, 136, 151, 160, 171, 173, 184, 199, 200, 201, 203, 219*

Bexar County Emergency Management *22, 49, 80*

Bexar County Exposition Hall *36, 51, 60, 76, 98, 117, 126, 127, 150, 151, 171, 186, 188*

Bexar County Hospital District *37, 200, 203*

Bexar County Medical Examiner *90*

BiblioTech *87, 92, 109, 110*

Biden, Joe *111, 113, 114, 130, 131, 155, 163, 164, 170, 178, 183, 189, 198, 204, 206, 208*

Biery, Judge Fred *65, 66*

Bieser, Kathy *87*

Bill Miller Barbecue *109*

Blanco Café *109*

Blue Star Arts *52*

Boyen, Craig *78*

Brehm, Cynthia *66*

Bridger, Dr. Colleen *48, 84, 86, 157, 158*

Brockhouse, Greg *139, 154*

Brodesky, Josh *10, 11, 158*

Brooke Army Medical Center 24
Brooks City Base 34, 160
Bugg, Bruce 99, 100
Burnett, Erin 29
Bush, George P. 148, 160
Business and Unemployment Committee 69
Califano, Jr., Joseph A. 56
Callanen, Jacque 30, 84, 154
Calvert, Tommy 69, 135, 136, 157
Cares Act 51
Carielo, Julissa 69
Carmilitas Mexican Restaurant 109
CAST Tech High School 87
Catholic Charities 151
CDC 19, 20, 26, 27-30, 48, 55, 56, 80, 83, 115, 119, 151, 156, 162, 168, 169, 174-176, 180, 186, 187, 189, 190, 192, 197, 198, 203, 205, 206, 209
Central Park 67, 194
Chauvin, Derek 71
Chloroquine 35, 36, 108
Clark, Troy 83
Clay-Flores, Rebeca 31, 89, 113, 132, 151-153, 157, 161
Club Giraud 79
CNN 29, 41, 44
Cole, Laura 109
Coleman, Kyle 89
Coltharp, Donna 182
Community Labs 100, 101, 201, 203
Community Response and Equity Coalition 154
Confluence Park 68
Cooper, Eric 58
Coronavirus Aid, Relief, and Economic Security Act. (CARES) 51, 69, 159
CPS Energy 32, 140, 142, 144, 145, 199
Criminal justice 73, 92, 135
Crocket Building 105
Curry, Dan 101

Daily Beast 228
Dallas Chaparrals 33
Dallas County 21
Daniels, Damian Lamar 96
Davenport, Cody 126
Davidson, Bruce 48, 50, 224
De Lai 64
DeBerry, Trish 30, 89, 113, 136, 152, 157, 160, 199
Delta variant 158, 162, 163, 165, 168, 169, 171, 175, 177, 178, 184, 188, 190, 192, 193, 195, 199, 201, 206, 213
Democratic Republic of the Congo 22
DePrisco, Thomas 43
Diamond Princess 21, 29, 48
Dinnin, Kevin 117
DNA 18, 52, 121, 122, 124
Duvoisin, Marc 158
Dyess, Glynn and Connie 133, 134
Eagles Court 92
Early voting 84, 85, 111-113
Ebola 22, 23, 25
Eckhardt, Judge Sarah 21
Economic Transition Committee 69
Edgewood School District 150
Eighmy, Taylor 98, 137, 191
El Paso County 21, 115
El Salvador 150
Election 20, 31, 65, 66, 77, 84, 85, 88, 89, 111-114, 139, 154, 181, 189, 222
Electric Reliability Council of Texas (ERCOT) 142
Elizondo, Paul 66
Elliott, Sean 73
Emerick, Dawn 48, 76, 83
Epley, Eric 23, 48, 49, 200-202
Erfurth, Nicole 49, 157
Esper, Mark 26
Espinoza, Dr. Rita 125
ESPN 140

Estesevimab 117

Facebook 131, 139, 155, 215

Fauci, Dr. Anthony 19, 35, 48, 53, 165

Federal and State Advocacy Committee 68

Federal Emergency Management
  Agency (FEMA) 84, 167

Federal Occupational Safety and
  Health Administration 183

Floyd, George 71

Food and Drug Administration (FDA) 30,
  35, 54, 108, 117, 118, 149, 166, 179, 186,
  189, 198, 210

Food Security and Shelter Committee 51,
  68, 69

Forbes, Bryn 73

Fort Worth Stock Show 127

Fox Tech

Fraudulent COVID-19 tests 54

Frederick's Bistro 109

Ft. Sam Houston 24, 25, 167, 168

Gaddafi, Muammar 30

Gager, Mark 40

Garcia-Siller, Archbishop Gustavo 173

Garza, Mayor Ed 34, 42

Gentry, Barbara 68

Giroir, Admiral Brett P. 26

Green, Phil 63

Guardian (United States Edition) 175

Guatemala 150

Guevara, Thomas 160

Guillain-Barre syndrome 56

Guillen, Juan 49

Gulf of Sidra 30

Gutierrez, Dr. Juan 61, 200

Hagee, John and Matthew 91

Hancock, Dr. Paul 90

Hardberger, Phil 67, 106, 148

Harris County 21

Harris, Kamala 131

Harvard University 37

Health Transition Committee 69

H-E-B 47, 78, 88, 107, 143, 181, 200

Heckler, Margaret 52

Hellerstedt, John 38

Hermann, Don 39

Hermann, Ron 39

Hernandez, George 24, 85, 119, 124, 128,
  157, 163, 164, 171, 196

Herriot, Jennifer 157

Hidalgo Foundation 72, 109

Hidalgo, Judge Lina 21

Hinojosa, Saul 100

HIV 25, 52, 53

Holiday Inn 27

Honduras 150

Hong Kong University of Science
  and Technology 64

Hood, Charles 48, 49

Houston Livestock and Rodeo 127

Howard, Derrick 150, 151, 153

H5NI avian-flu 17

Hydroxychloroquine 35, 36, 108

International Bank of Commerce (IBC) 63

J. Alexander's Restaurant 79, 109

Jenkins, Clay 21

Jim's Restaurant 109

Johnson & Johnson (J&J) 186, 192

Joint Base San Antonio-Lackland 20, 48

KENS 158

Kidd, W. Nim 167

KLRN 158

Krier, Judge Cyndi Taylor 33, 139, 140

Kronkosky Foundation 99

KSAT 158

Kurian, Dr. Anita 157, 205

Kwok-Young, Dr. Yuen 64

Labor Day 97, 98

La Coronela 109

La Paloma 109

Lackland Air Force Base 20, 27, 29, 48

LeBlanc Burley, Jelynne 46
Loeffler, Nancy 126
Longoria, Judge John 32
Los Barrios 109
Lowes Home Improvement 81, 82
Lozito, Mike 92
Luther, William 10
Massachusetts 168, 175, 221
Mandell, Elliot 124
Martinez, Mario 157
Martinez, Pedro 178, 203
Mayorkas, Alejandro 163, 164
McConnell, Mitch 131
McCurley, Jane 174
Medicaid 117, 118, 175, 181, 183
Medicare 175, 181, 183
Medici, Mark 158
Meissonier, Nancy 19, 27
Memorial Day 70, 71, 76, 98
Merck and Ridgeback Biotherapeutics
  185, 216
Middle East Respiratory Syndrome
  (MERS) 16, 19
Methodist Health Care 90
Methodist Hospital 174, 175
Mexico 115, 150, 190,
Migrant Center 150-152
Minneapolis Police Department 71
Mission Reach 67
Mission San Jose 106, 136
Mitchell, Seth 37, 57, 157
Moderna 118, 122, 130, 169, 186, 192, 215
Molina, Dr. Kimberly 90
Molnupiravir 185, 198
mRNA 122, 186, 192, 194, 215, 216, 225,
  216, 228
N95 mask 39, 61
Najim, Harvey 68
National Basketball Association (NBA) 33
National Center for Health Statistics 210

National Football League (NFL) 134, 145,
  146, 228
National Institute of Virology 17
National Security Collaboration 137
NCAA Basketball 139, 140
New England Journal of Medicine 202
New York 40, 170, 193, 202
New York City 42, 43, 67, 193, 194
New York Times 10, 166, 170, 222, 229
New York Yankees 70
Newsom, Gavin 184, 185
Nicha's Comida Mexicana 106, 109
Nirenberg, Ron 9, 12, 20, 21, 23, 24, 26-29,
  32, 34-36, 38, 41, 42, 44, 45, 46, 48-51,
  54, 55, 58, 60-62, 64, 66, 68, 70, 72, 73,
  74, 76-80, 84, 85, 87, 88, 90, 91, 94, 95,
  97 98, 101, 102, 106, 112-117, 120, 122,
  124, 125, 128, 132, 133, 137-141, 143,
  144-148, 154, 156-159, 161, 163, 165,
  166, 169-171, 174, 176, 178, 182, 184,
  189, 196, 197, 199-203, 206, 207, 213,
  214, 218, 224
Nixon, Dennis 63
North Star Mall 27
North East Independent School District
  (NEISD) 180, 187
Northside Independent School District
  (NISD) 59, 60, 99, 149, 150, 180, 187,
  212
Obama, Barack 41, 208
Omicron 192, 193, 195-199, 202, 204-206,
  209, 210, 212, 213, 221
Operation Warp Speed 51
Opioid 53, 54, 79
OxyContin 53
Pam's 87, 109
Paper ballots 111
Patrick, Dan 41, 148, 152, 160
Paxlovid 186, 198
Paxton, Ken 64, 65, 91, 176, 183, 184

Pelaez, Manny 69
Pelosi, Nancy 131
Pence, Mike 130, 131
Pershing Jr. High School, Houston, Texas 133
Personal protective equipment (PPE) 26, 39, 211
Pew Research Center 71
Pfizer 118, 122, 138, 178, 186, 189, 192, 198, 202, 215, 216
Philadelphia 32
Phillips, Bill 128, 163, 164
Plaza de Armas 29, 49, 103, 104
Polymerase Chain Reaction test (PCR) 36, 37, 100, 149, 201, 203
Popovich, Gregg 120, 130
Prosper, Erika 143
QAnon 156
Quidel's Quick-Vue test 149
Quiroz, Joe 49
Ramos, Monica 37, 49, 157, 224
Rangel, Judge Ron 32
Reagan, Ronald 19
Red Cross 96
Reed, Susan 43
REGEN-COV 108, 171
Remdesivir 108, 201
Respiratory syncytial virus (RSV) 169, 180
Richardson, Lt. General Laura J. 167, 168
Rickhoff, Tom 89
Rio Grande River 151
Rivard, Bob 158
Rivera, James 47, 114, 224
RK Catering 151
RNA 121, 122
Roberson, Larry 28, 78, 79, 170, 171, 174
Robert B. Green Clinic 164
Robinson, Tony 167
Robinson, Riley 123
Rodriguez, Justin 69, 107, 111, 136, 163, 170, 193

Rodriguez, Sergio "Chico" 31, 69, 89
Roy, Chip 26
Sako, Dr. Edward 110
Salazar, Sheriff Javier 73, 81, 151, 197
Samaniego, Judge Ricardo 21, 115
San Antonio Chamber of Commerce 112, 188
San Antonio Express-News 10, 68, 127, 148, 158, 182, 187, 194, 229
San Antonio Fire Department 36
San Antonio Food Bank 10, 11, 58, 60, 69
San Antonio Football Club 33, 34
San Antonio Livestock Exposition (SALE) 126, 127
San Antonio Metropolitan Health District 24, 229
San Antonio Missions baseball 33
San Antonio Parks Foundation 128
San Antonio Police Department (SAPD) 97
San Antonio Report 158, 229
San Antonio River 66, 67
San Antonio School Independent School District (SAISD) 178, 180, 202, 212
San Antonio Sports Association 33
San Antonio Spurs 33, 34, 73, 120, 126, 130, 173
San Antonio Water System (SAWS) 144, 145
San Pedro Creek 68, 103, 105, 137
Sandoval, Ana 69
Santa Rosa Hospital 25, 86
SARS 15-18, 64, 228
Schlesinger, Larry 25, 96
Segovia, Andy 28, 170
Sencer, David 56
Shelby, Richard 26
Silos Restaurant 109
Singer, Paul 79
Smith, David 48, 78, 97, 157, 159, 177, 193
Social Services Committee 51, 68, 69

Somerset High School *100*

Sosa, Jose *110*

South Texas Blood and Tissue Center *100*

South Texas Medical Center *122*

Southwest Texas Regional Advisory Council
  (STRAC) *23, 48, 49, 200-202, 229*

Spectrum News/Ipsos *178*

St. Louis *32*

St. Mary's University *182*

STAAR test *150*

Stay Home, Work Safe *40, 45, 46, 55, 61,
  144, 210*

Strain, Pam and David *87*

Sun Harvest Natural Food supermarkets *39*

Tamiflu *185*

Target *88*

Tarrant County *21*

Taylor, Dr. Barbara *69, 225*

Taylor, Ivy *34*

Telemundo *158*

Teniente-Matson, Dr. Cynthia *99*

Texas A&M-San Antonio *99*

Texas Alcohol Beverage Commission
  (TABC) *108*

Texas Biomedical Research Institute
  (Texas BioMed) *22, 25, 96, 216*

Texas Federation for Advanced
  Manufacturing *166*

Texas Freedom Force *71*

Texas Monthly 79, 229

Texas National Guard *111*

Texas Supreme Court *66, 84, 174, 176,
  177, 180*

Thanksgiving *42, 102, 116, 120*

The Palm *109*

Thompson, Dr. Ian *86*

Thompson, Toni *203*

Tobin Foundation *99*

Tony G's *109, 151*

Toyota Field *34*

Trader's Village *58*

Travis County *21*

Travis Park *73*

Traylor, Jeff *191*

Treviño, Roberto *69*

Trump, Donald *15, 19, 31, 35, 36, 39, 41,
  42, 44, 45, 48, 51, 65, 66, 84, 88, 107, 108,
  111-114, 116, 120, 127, 128, 130, 131,
  156, 175, 181, 185, 198, 204, 205, 208,
  221, 222*

U.S. Department of Defense *27*

U.S. Department of Health and Human
  Services *26, 165, 220*

U.S. Department of Homeland Security
  40, 44, 151, 163, 164

UC Berkeley's International Science
  Institute *64*

United Soccer League (USL) *33*

University Health System (UHS) *24, 28,
  57, 85, 107, 129, 143, 148, 163, 164, 171,
  181, 189, 195, 196, 201, 206, 216, 217,
  225, 229*

University of Texas at San Antonio
  (UTSA) *24, 61, 104, 137, 138, 191, 200,
  230*

University of Texas Health Science Center
  (UT Health) *24, 25, 28, 37, 69, 164, 187,
  216, 225, 230*

Univision *158*

USAA *32, 173*

USS *Mahan* 30

UTSA School of Data Science *137*

Val Verde County *82*

Valero *33, 151*

Veltman, Hap *52*

VIA Metropolitan Transit *45, 46, 113*

Voelkel, Kevin *69*

Walker, Lonnie *73*

Wall Street Journal 173, 215, 218, 220, 230

Walmart *88, 143*

Walsh, Erik 48, 83, 176, 177
Washington Post 44, 230
Washington, George 179
Watts, Mikal 79
WellMed Clinic 164
Wells, Tullos 99
Wendland, Paul and Ben 127
Weston, Graham 99, 137
Whitley, Judge Glenn 21
Wickerham, Kristopher 87
Williams, Reed 145
WOAI 158
Wolff, Kevin 30, 42, 69
Wolff, Matthew and Molly 47, 195
Wolff, Tracy 42, 46, 47, 51, 52, 72, 87, 93,
    127, 135, 138, 142, 144, 182, 187, 190,
    191, 193-195, 198

Women's Final Four basketball
    championship 139
Wonderland Mall 128, 129, 133, 138, 143,
    148, 154, 163, 164, 186, 189, 200, 201,
    203, 216
Woo, Dr. Junda 90, 177
Woods, Brian 59, 99, 149, 180
Woolworth Building 105, 106, 148
World Health Organization (WHO) 18,
    192, 230
World Trade Center 42, 43
Wuhan, China 15-18, 20, 21, 204
XTC Cabaret 116
Yokohama 21
Zhenbgli, Dr. Shi 17
Zuckerberg, Mark 155

By the same author:

The Changing Face of San Antonio:
An Insider's View of an Emerging International City

Transforming San Antonio:
An Insider's View to the AT&T Arena, Toyota, the PGA Village
and the Riverwalk Extension

Bexar BiblioTech:
The Evolution of the Country's First All-digital Public Library

Baseball for Real Men

Seven Spiritual Laws for Senior Players

Mayor:
An Inside View of San Antonio Politics, 1981-1995

Photo by Alexis Velasquez

Nelson Wolff has served the greater San Antonio area as a member of the Texas House of Representatives, the Texas Senate in 1973, and the San Antonio City Council, as well as mayor of San Antonio. He currently serves as Bexar County Judge, a position to which he was appointed to in 2001 and to which he has been elected five times. During his almost 50-year tenure as a public servant, Wolff has played a key role in countless economic and community development initiatives.